Best Easy Day Hikes
Lake Tahoe

Help Us Keep This Guide Up to Date

Every effort has been made by the author and editors to make this guide as accurate and useful as possible. However, many things can change after a guide is published—trails are rerouted, regulations change, facilities come under new management, etc.

We would love to hear from you concerning your experiences with this guide and how you feel it could be improved and kept up to date. While we may not be able to respond to all comments and suggestions, we'll take them to heart and we'll also make certain to share them with the author. Please send your comments and suggestions to the following address:

> Globe Pequot Press
> Reader Response/Editorial Department
> P.O. Box 480
> Guilford, CT 06437

Or you may e-mail us at:

> editorial@GlobePequot.com

Thanks for your input, and happy trails!

Best Easy Day Hikes Series

Best Easy Day Hikes
Lake Tahoe

Second Edition

Tracy Salcedo-Chourré

FALCONGUIDES

GUILFORD, CONNECTICUT
HELENA, MONTANA
AN IMPRINT OF GLOBE PEQUOT PRESS

FALCONGUIDES®

FalconGuides is an imprint of Globe Pequot Press.
Falcon, FalconGuides, and Outfit Your Mind are registered trademarks
of Morris Book Publishing, LLC.

Project editor: Gregory Hyman
Layout: Kevin Mak
Maps: Off Route Inc. © Morris Book Publishing, LLC

TOPO! Explorer software and SuperQuad source maps courtesy of
National Geographic Maps. For information about TOPO! Explorer,
TOPO!, and Nat Geo Maps products, go to www.topo.com or www
.natgeomaps.com.

Library of Congress Cataloging-in-Publication Data
Salcedo-Chourré, Tracy.
  Best easy day hikes, Lake Tahoe / Tracy Salcedo-Chourré. – 2nd ed.
    p. cm.
  Includes bibliographical references and index.
  ISBN 978-0-7627-5253-9 (alk. paper) 1. Hiking—Tahoe, Lake,
Region (Calif. and Nev.)—Guidebooks. 2. Tahoe, Lake, Region (Calif.
and Nev.)—Guidebooks. I. Title.
  GV199.42.T16S35 2010
  917.94'38-dc22
                                               2009049360

Printed in the United States of America

10 9 8 7 6 5 4 3 2 1

To the Friedman and Rodman families

Contents

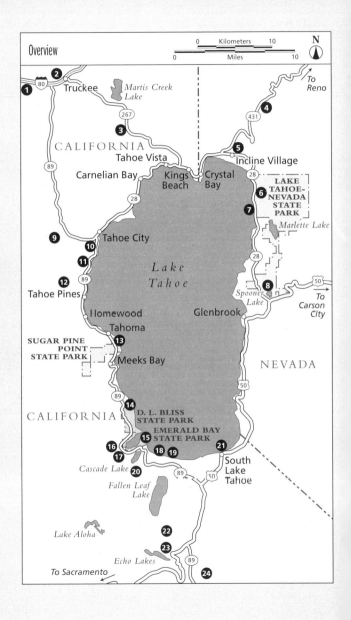

Kilometers
Miles

N

To Reno

Truckee

Martis Creek Lake

267

CALIFORNIA

Tahoe Vista

Carnelian Bay

Kings Beach

Crystal Bay

Incline Village

431

LAKE TAHOE-NEVADA STATE PARK

Marlette Lake

28

Lake Tahoe

Tahoe City

Tahoe Pines

89

Homewood

Tahoma

Glenbrook

Spooner Lake

50

To Carson City

SUGAR PINE POINT STATE PARK

Meeks Bay

NEVADA

89

50

CALIFORNIA

D. L. BLISS STATE PARK

EMERALD BAY STATE PARK

South Lake Tahoe

Cascade Lake

Fallen Leaf Lake

89

50

Lake Aloha

Echo Lakes

89

To Sacramento

Acknowledgments

Thanks to the following folks for their advice and help with the first edition of this guide: Mike St. Michel and Don Lane of the USDA Forest Service–Lake Tahoe Basin Management Unit; Dave Nettle of Alpenglow Sports in Tahoe City; Gisela Steiner of Tahoe Trail Trekkers; Bill Schneider; editors David Lee, Charlene Patterson, and Erica Olsen; and George Meyers, who helped get it all started right after the twins were born.

Thanks to these folks for help and review of the second edition: Don Lane and Lindsay Gusses of the Lake Tahoe Basin Management Unit; Mark Kimbrough, executive director of the Tahoe Rim Trail Association; Hal Paris and Pandora Bahlman of the Incline Village General Improvement District; Roger Adamson, park superintendent of the Tahoe City Public Utility District; Bill Houdyschell of the forestry division of the Tahoe Donner Association; Bill Champion of Lake Tahoe–Nevada State Park; Dean Lutz, Jeff Wiley, and Susanne Jensen of Tahoe National Forest; and Jacqui Zink, park ranger with the U.S. Army Corps of Engineers at Martis Creek Lake.

Thanks to these folks for everything: Howard and Rita Friedman and their family, especially Mitchell and Tory; Jesse and Judy Salcedo; Chris Salcedo and Angela Jones; Nick and Nancy Salcedo; Sarah Chourré; my awesome sons, Cruz, Jesse, and Penn; and my husband, Martin Chourré.

Introduction

Writers have been hurling superlatives at Lake Tahoe with the earnestness of Little League pitchers for hundreds of years. The great blue deep just swallows them up. Even legendary naturalist John Muir gave it a shot: Reflecting on Sierran lakes, he mused, "Of these glacial gems, Lake Tahoe is King of them all . . ."

True but . . . well, sorry, Mr. Muir. Even you, like the rest of us, fall short. Tahoe is too perfect to be adequately captured by overused adjectives and strained metaphors. Better to consider the lake quietly, from a trail that skims its shoreline or looks down on it from above.

People have been drawn to the lake for thousands of years. First there were the Washoe, who gathered the bounty of summer on the water and from its rim. Next came the Europeans, first Spaniards and then American fortune hunters, who scoured the high country for mineral wealth. These days, folks gather winter and summer to enjoy short holidays or to make the blue heart of the Sierra their home. Invariably they end up outside, lured by the dramatic landscape into the fresh pine-scented air. Invariably they want to take a hike.

This guide has been compiled to showcase Lake Tahoe and its environs. Even when it's not visible, the lake informs each trail, if only by proximity. Selecting the "best" day hikes presented a conundrum—how to choose from so many awesome options? Then again, how could I go wrong? The trick has been to pick hikes that satisfy visitor and lucky resident alike, to include something for everyone. Thus these hikes range from super-short wheelchair-accessible interpretive trails to thigh-burning treks to high-altitude viewpoints. Some routes are ideal for adventure, some for contemplation. Others are perfect for a Sunday afternoon outing with the family, and yet others for winding down on a summer evening after a hard day's work.

To walk in the mountains, whether along a narrow path that delves into wilderness or on a well-kept paved trail, is, I believe, to renew the soul. I hope that anyone who embarks on a journey into Tahoe's natural world will find the peace and inspiration that I have found there. Get out, take a hike, and let your stunned, reverent silence describe Tahoe's beauty for you.

The Nature of Tahoe

Tahoe's trails range from rugged and mountainous to flat and paved. Hikes in this guide cover the gamut. While by definition a best easy day hike poses little danger to the traveler, knowing a few details about the nature of the Lake Tahoe region will enhance your explorations.

Weather

Tahoe's hiking season generally stretches from the first of May to the end of October, with trails at lower elevations melting off before those at higher elevations. When the trails open is dependent on the amount of winter snowfall and the speed of the snowmelt.

High temperatures in spring and fall range from the low 50s to the high 60s. In July, August, and September, temperatures jump into the high 70s and 80s, with occasional hot spells. Overnight lows are in the 30s and 40s.

Afternoon thunderstorms are fairly common in the summer months and taper off by autumn. Be prepared for changeable weather—rain, cold, or heat—by wearing layers and packing waterproof gear.

Critters
Black bear encounters usually involve some kind of food, whether left in a car, a tent, a garbage can, or on a windowsill. They've been known to rip windshields out of automobiles to get at coolers and to stroll through the open doors of homes to rummage in refrigerators. If you encounter a bear on the trail, do not run: Stand still and make noise, and the bear will generally scram. Never come between a mama bear and her cubs; if you see cubs, leave the area immediately.

Be Prepared

Hikers should be prepared for any situation, whether they are out for a short stroll along the Truckee River or venturing into the alpine heights of the Desolation Wilderness. Some specific advice:

- Know the basics of first aid, including how to treat bleeding, bites and stings, and fractures, strains, or sprains. Pack a first-aid kit on each excursion.

- Familiarize yourself with the symptoms and treatment of altitude sickness (especially if you are visiting from a significantly lesser altitude). If you or one of your party exhibits any symptom of this condition, including headache, nausea, or unusual fatigue, descend to a lower altitude immediately and seek medical attention.

- Know the symptoms of both cold- and heat-related conditions, including hypothermia and heat stroke. The best way to avoid these afflictions is to wear appropriate clothing, drink lots of water, eat enough to keep the internal fires properly stoked, and keep a pace that is within your physical limits.

- Regardless of the weather, your body needs a lot of water while hiking. Drinking a full 32-ounce bottle on each outing is a good idea no matter how short the hike, but more is always better.

- Don't drink from streams, rivers, creeks, or lakes without treating or filtering the water first. Waterways and water bodies may host a variety of contaminants, including giardia, which can cause serious intestinal unrest.

- The sun at these altitudes (all of these hikes are above 5,000 feet) can be brutal, so wear a strong sunscreen.

- Afternoon and evening thunderstorms harbor a host of potential hazards, including rain, hail, and lightning. Retreat to the safety of the car or other shelter if you suspect the weather will turn, and carry protective clothing.

- Prepare for extremes of both heat and cold by dressing in layers.

- Carry a backpack in which you can store extra clothing, ample drinking water and food, and whatever goodies, like guidebooks, cameras, and binoculars, you might want.

- Some trails have cell phone coverage. Bring your device, but make sure it's turned off or on the vibrate setting. Nothing like a "wake the dead"-loud ring to startle every creature in the area, including fellow hikers.

- Watch children carefully. Waterways move deceptively fast, animals and plants may harbor danger, and rocky terrain and cliffs are potential hazards. Children should carry a plastic whistle; if they become lost, they should stay in one place and blow the whistle to summon help.

Zero Impact

Trails around Lake Tahoe are heavily used. We, as trail users and advocates, must be especially vigilant to make sure our passage leaves no lasting mark. Here are some basic guidelines for preserving trails in the region:

- Pack out all trash, including biodegradable items like orange peels. You might also pack out garbage left by less considerate hikers.

- Avoid damaging trailside soils and plants by remaining on the established route. Social trails contribute to erosion problems, damage fragile alpine environments, and create unsightly scars on the landscape. Don't cut switchbacks, which also promotes erosion.

- Don't approach or feed any wild creatures—they are best able to survive if they remain self-reliant.

- Don't pick wildflowers or gather rocks, antlers, feathers, and other treasures along the trail. Removing these items will only take away from the next hiker's experience.

- Be courteous by not making loud noises while hiking.

- Many of these trails are multiuse, which means you'll share them with other hikers, trail runners, mountain bikers, and equestrians. Familiarize yourself with the proper trail etiquette, yielding the trail when appropriate.

- If possible, use outhouses at trailheads or along the trail. If not, pack in a lightweight trowel so that you can bury your waste 6 to 8 inches deep. Pack out used toilet paper in a plastic bag. Make sure you relieve yourself at least 300 feet away from any surface water or boggy spot.

- Wilderness permits are required, even for day hikers, if you plan to enter the Desolation, Mount Rose, or Granite Chief Wildernesses. Permits are free and available at trailheads.

- Dogs are not permitted on state beaches or in any wilderness around Lake Tahoe. Dog beaches are available.

Getting Around Lake Tahoe

All hikes in this guide are within an hour's drive of one of the bigger little towns around Lake Tahoe. Tahoe City, Incline Village, and South Lake Tahoe/Stateline are used as touchstones for directions to trailheads. A scenic highway, variously designated CA 89, CA 28, NV 28, and US 50, circumnavigates the lake. All trailhead directions are given from this road.

Maps

The USGS quad is listed for every hike. If the hike is so short or well defined that no map is necessary, or if an adequate map is provided at the trailhead by the land manager, that is noted in its description.

The USDA Forest Service's Lake Tahoe Basin Management Unit map, available at forest service visitor centers and from retail outlets around the lake, is an excellent resource. The map is also online at www.fs.fed.us/r5/ltbmu/maps/index.shtml.

The Tom Harrison Recreation Map of Lake Tahoe also includes most of the hikes in this guide. For more informa-

tion call (415) 456-7940 or visit www.tomharrisonmaps
.com.

Public Transportation

Tahoe Area Regional Transit (TART) provides public transportation for north Lake Tahoe. For information on routes
and fares, call (530) 550-1212 or (800) 736-6365, or visit
www.placer.ca.gov/departments/works/transit/TART.aspx.

The South Tahoe Area Transit Authority's BlueGO
provides public transportation around Tahoe's South Shore.
For more information call (530) 541-7149 or visit www
.bluego.org.

Regional Trails

Hop onto any leg of the 165-mile-long **Tahoe Rim Trail
(TRT)** and you're guaranteed a great hike with an awesome
destination and sublime views of Lake Tahoe. The multiuse
trail encircles the entire lake, with trailheads in easy-to-
reach locations, and is the result of more than twenty-five
years of work by volunteers and land managers. For more
information contact the Tahoe Rim Trail Association, 948
Incline Way, Incline Village, NV 89451; (775) 298-0233;
www.tahoerimtrail.org.

The **Pacific Crest Trail (PCT)** is a wilderness enthu-
siast's dream. Riding the high ground for 2,650 miles
from the Canadian border in Washington to the deserts
of California bordering Mexico, this National Scenic Trail
provides ample ground for hikers to see America as few
ever can. No bikes or motorized vehicles are allowed on
the PCT. For more information contact the Pacific Crest
Trail Association, 250 Date Ave., Suite L, Sacramento, CA
95841; (916) 349-2109; www.pcta.org.

Land Management

The following government agencies manage public lands described in this guide and can provide further information on these hikes and other trails in their service areas.

- USDA Forest Service–Lake Tahoe Basin Management Unit, Forest Supervisor's Office, 35 College Dr., South Lake Tahoe, CA 96150; (530) 543-2600; www.fs.fed.us/r5/ltbmu

- USDA Forest Service–Lake Tahoe Basin Management Unit, North Tahoe Forest Service Office, 3080 North Lake Blvd., Tahoe City, CA 96145; (530) 583-3593; www.fs.fed.us/r5/ltbmu

- Nevada Division of State Parks, Lake Tahoe–Nevada State Park, P.O. Box 8867, Incline Village, NV 89452; (775) 831-0494; www.parks.nv.gov/lt.htm

- Humboldt-Toiyabe National Forest, Carson Ranger District, 1536 South Carson St., Carson City, Nevada 89701; (775) 882-2766; www.fs.fed.us/r4/htnf

How to Use This Guide

This guide is designed to be simple and easy to use. Each hike is described with a map and summary information that delivers the trail's vital statistics including length, difficulty, fees and permits, park hours, canine compatibility, and trail contacts. Directions to the trailhead are provided. Information about what you'll see along the trail, as well as tidbits about the natural and cultural history of the route, is given in the hike description. A detailed route finder (Miles and Directions) sets forth mileages between significant landmarks along the trail.

How the Hikes Were Chosen

Hikes chosen for this guide range in difficulty from flat excursions perfect for a family outing to more challenging treks to highland lakes. I've selected hikes all around the lake and in surrounding communities like Truckee and Tahoe Donner, so wherever your starting point you'll find an easy day hike nearby.

While these trails are among the best, keep in mind that other trails nearby may offer options better suited to your needs. Potential alternatives are suggested in the Options section at the end of hike descriptions.

Several good hikes that appeared in the first edition of this guide were bumped to make room for wonderful alternative trails. These excluded routes, along with summary information about how to reach them, are listed in the Options section of the nearest hike.

Selecting a Hike

These are all easy hikes, but "easy" is a relative term. Some would argue that no hike involving any kind of climbing is easy, but around Lake Tahoe climbs are a fact of life. Keep in mind that what you think is easy is entirely dependent on your level of fitness and the adequacy of your gear (primarily shoes). Use the trail's length as a gauge of its relative difficulty—even if climbing is involved, it won't be bad if the hike is less than 1 mile long. In addition to listing hikes that might appeal to the hiker seeking a certain experience, the Trail Finder lists the trails by level of difficulty. If you are hiking with a group, select a hike that's appropriate for the least fit and prepared in your party.

Approximate hiking times are based on the assumption that on flat ground, most walkers average 2 miles per hour. Adjust that rate by the steepness of the terrain and your level of fitness (subtract time if you're an aerobic animal and add time if you're hiking with kids), and you have a ballpark hiking duration. Be sure to add more time if you plan to picnic or take part in other activities like bird-watching or photography.

Trail Finder

Best Hikes for Lake Lovers

- 7 Skunk Harbor
- 8 Spooner Lake Loop
- 15 Vikingsholm and Emerald Point
- 23 Pacific Crest Trail at Echo Lakes

Best Hikes for River Lovers

- 3 Martis Creek Wildlife Area
- 10 Truckee River Trail

Best Hikes for Great Views

- 12 Ellis Peak Trail
- 17 Cascade Falls

Best Hikes for Nature Lovers

- 2 Northwoods Nature Trail at Tahoe Donner
- 4 Tahoe Meadows Interpretive Trail
- 11 Page Meadows

Best Hikes for Children

- 6 Sand Point Nature Trail
- 18 Rainbow Trail
- 22 Angora Lakes

Best Hikes for History Lovers

- 14 The Lighthouse and Rubicon Point
- 15 Vikingsholm and Emerald Point
- 19 Lake of the Sky Trail and Tallac Historic Site

Best Hikes for a Workout

- 5 Incline Village Exercise Course

| 13 | General Creek Loop at Sugar Pine Point State Park |
| 9 | Five Lakes Trail |

Hike Ratings

(Hikes are listed from easiest to most challenging.)

6	Sand Point Nature Trail
18	Rainbow Trail
5	Incline Village Exercise Course
4	Tahoe Meadows Interpretive Trail
2	Northwoods Nature Trail at Tahoe Donner
21	Lam Watah Nature Trail
1	Lakeside Interpretive Trail at Donner Lake
22	Angora Lakes
8	Spooner Lake Loop
19	Lake of the Sky Trail and Tallac Historic Site
24	Tahoe Rim Trail at Big Meadows
23	Pacific Crest Trail at Echo Lakes
3	Martis Creek Wildlife Area
13	General Creek Loop at Sugar Pine Point State Park
10	Truckee River Trail
16	Eagle Lake
17	Cascade Falls
7	Skunk Harbor
11	Page Meadows
15	Vikingsholm and Emerald Point
14	The Lighthouse and Rubicon Point
20	Cathedral Lake
9	Five Lakes Trail
12	Ellis Peak Trail

Map Legend

=8=	Interstate Highway
=19=	U.S. Highway
=34=	State Highway
══	Local Road
== == ==	Unpaved Road
▬▬▬▬▬	Featured Trail
- - - - -	Trail
▌▌▌▌▌▌▌	Boardwalk
- ·· - ·· -	State Line
～	River/Creek
⬭	Body of Water
⥿	Marsh/Swamp
⸽ ⸽	State Park/Wilderness Area
⊟	Bench
⛵	Boat Launch
⌣⌣	Bridge
⛺	Camping
•—•	Gate
❷	Information Center
🕯	Lighthouse
🅿	Parking
▲	Peak
🖾	Picnic Area
■	Point of Interest/Structure
🚻	Restroom
○	Town
⓫	Trailhead
🖼	Viewpoint/Overlook
≷	Waterfall

1 Lakeside Interpretive Trail at Donner Lake

Lake Tahoe gets all the glory, but this satellite lake, likewise deep and blue, hosts a wonderful interpretive trail that focuses attention not only on the spectacular setting but also on the remarkable history of the infamous pass that shares its name.

Distance: 2.4 miles out and back
Approximate hiking time: 2 hours
Difficulty: Easy
Trail surface: Dirt singletrack
Best seasons: Spring, summer, fall
Other trail users: None
Canine compatibility: Leashed dogs permitted
Fees and permits: Day-use fee to enter the park. Free parking is available along Donner Pass Road outside the park. To reach the trailhead from the free parking area, follow the park road to the picnic area lot.
Schedule: Park hours vary with the season. Visitor center hours are 9:00 a.m. to 5:00 p.m. daily in summer; 9:00 a.m. to 4:00 p.m. after Labor Day.

Maps: USGS Truckee and Norden (CA); park trail map available at the entrance station and on an information board at the entrance
Other: While at the park you can visit the Emigrant Trail Museum (open from 9:00 a.m. to 4:00 p.m. daily); the Pioneer Monument; and the Murphy family cabin site (a remnant of the Donner Party). Contact ReserveAmerica (800-444-7275; www.reserveamerica.com) for camping reservations.
Trail contact: Donner Memorial State Park, 12593 Donner Pass Rd., Truckee, CA 96161; (530) 582-7892; www.parks.ca.gov or www.donnermemorial.org

Finding the trailhead: From Lake Tahoe's North Shore, take CA 89 from Tahoe City or CA 28 from Kings Beach to I-80. Head west on I-80 to the Donner Pass Road exit (about 0.7 mile west of the CA 89 interchange). Go left (south) on Donner Pass Road to the well-signed park entrance on the left (south). The trailhead is in the parking lot for the picnic area. Follow the park road past the entrance station and across the bridge, staying right at the gated campground road, to the lot. Restrooms, picnic facilities, and camping are available. GPS: N39 19.415' / W120 14.220'

The Hike

Who hasn't heard of the Donner Party? Trapped by deep snow below the summit of what would become known as Donner Pass in the winter of 1846–47, these embattled emigrants—they'd already encountered a number of hardships on their cross-country passage—endured madness, despair, and cannibalism in their fight to survive. More than thirty souls perished in the scattering of cabins and camps the travelers established around Donner Lake, with two cabin sites within the park boundaries.

No worries of such trauma on this hike, however—it's barely long or arduous enough to bring on hunger for a handful of trail mix. It also helps satisfy any curiosity about how this rugged country was eventually tamed, with interpretive panels describing settlement and industry in the area and the construction of the railroad and highway that would finally make travel over the pass easy even in winter.

The interpretive part of the trail is located at the west end, and if you pay the entrance fee, you can park at the beach at China Cove and hike back toward the entrance station. It's described here beginning at the picnic area at the Donner Creek dam, with easy access from parking outside the park.

Lakeside Interpretive Trail at Donner Lake

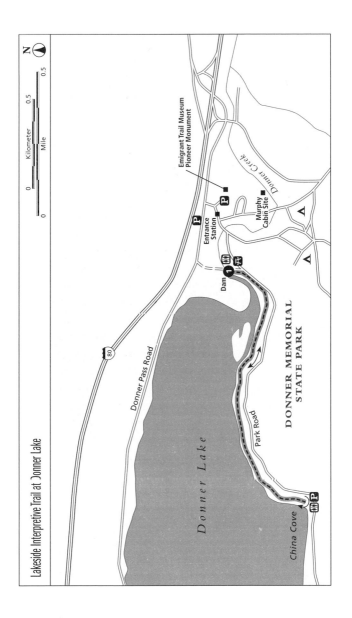

The trail begins at a small sign near the gauging station on Donner Creek, with the blue-green lake welling up alongside the dirt track. It roughly parallels the park road, with access to lakeside beaches, picnic grounds, and restrooms along most of its length. Expect some road noise from the nearby interstate and the park road—and the occasional rumble and whistle blow of a train riding high on the mountainside to the south—but you'll also be able to hear birds chirping in the lakeside brambles and the wind whirring through the treetops.

Tile mosaics touting the benefits of recycling, healthy forests, and responsible development, created by local fifth-graders, decorate the trailside at the 0.3-mile mark. The open forest allows glimpses of the gray granite heights of Donner Peak and Schallenberger Ridge to the south and west. A chain of picnic areas begins with a prime spot on a spit of sand on the southeast shore of the lake, with views across the water to lakeshore cabins on the north side.

The interpretive signs begin here too, focusing on the human and natural history of the area. From how fire helps maintain forest health to the geologic origins of the Sierra Nevada; from the lives of the Native Americans that summered in the area to the lives of early European settlers; from construction of a wagon road over the pass in the 1850s to the completion of the interstate in the 1960s—it's covered on the signs.

China Cove's crescent beach, with great views across the lake to the western peaks and ridges, is at trail's end. Picnic tables and restrooms make this the perfect place for lunch and relaxing. Return as you came (the most scenic route) or follow the park road back to the trailhead.

Miles and Directions

0.0   Start at the trail sign near the gauging station, heading southwest on the waterside path.

0.3   Pass tile mosaics.

0.5   Pass a picnic site on a sand spit, then continue past a series of picnic sites on the left (south) side of the trail.

1.2   Reach the beach at China Cove, take a break, then retrace your steps to the trailhead.

2.4   Arrive back at the trailhead.

2 Northwoods Nature Trail at Tahoe Donner

The meadows and woodlands surrounding Tahoe Donner provide a peaceful setting for this interpretive nature trail. The boardwalk section is particularly inviting, with wildflowers flourishing in late spring and summer.

Distance: 2.1-mile loop
Approximate hiking time: 1 hour
Difficulty: Easy
Trail surface: Singletrack; boardwalk
Best seasons: Late spring, summer, fall
Other trail users: None
Canine compatibility: Leashed dogs permitted
Fees and permits: None
Schedule: Sunrise to sunset daily

Maps: USGS Truckee (CA); Tahoe Donner Association Trail Map available at the trailhead; nature trail interpretive guide and trail map available at www.tahoedonner.com
Trail contact: Tahoe Donner Association Member Services Office, 11509 Northwoods Blvd., Truckee, CA 96161; (530) 587-9400; www.tahoedonner.com

Finding the trailhead: From Lake Tahoe take either CA 89 from Tahoe City or CA 28 from Kings Beach to I-80. Head west on I-80 to the Donner Pass Road exit (about 0.7 mile west of the CA 89 interchange). Go right (east) on Donner Pass Road for 0.4 mile to Northwoods Boulevard. Turn left (north) onto Northwoods Boulevard and go 1.4 miles to the Northwoods Clubhouse and parking lot on the right (east). The signed trailhead is in the northwest corner of the clubhouse parking lot. Restrooms, information, and a variety of recreational and picnic opportunities are available at the clubhouse. GPS: N39 20.624' / W120 12.991'

The Hike

Though it may be buggy, a visit to the meadow and wetland surrounding Trout Creek in late spring and early summer, when the wildflowers are in bloom, puts a fine topper on this winning hike. Mule ear with huge fuzzy leaves surrounding sunburst yellow flowers, red penstemon, delicate purple shooting stars, thimbleberries with tiny white flowers and big, broad leaves, wild rose with fragile pink blossoms—they all thrive along the creek and nature trail.

The nature trail is part of an extensive trail system in the Tahoe Donner development on the north side of the Truckee River valley. Though houses are sprinkled among the trees and the trail never wanders far from Northwoods Boulevard, the subdivision's main road, the area takes great pride in its natural setting and recreational opportunities. The trail is well maintained and features a series of boardwalks and bridges that wind through the most fragile parts of the riparian zone.

Interpretative stations and signage are thorough and well done. The Tahoe Donner Association has produced a wonderful guide with detailed entries on flora, fauna, and history keyed to numbered stations along the trail. No worries if you don't have the naturalist guide: Interpretive signs along the track inform about bears and birds of prey, wildflowers and willows, trout and trees. White blazes on the trees also mark the route.

As with all loops, you can travel this one in either direction, but it is described clockwise. A gentle climb on a singletrack path leads to the meadow and riparian area, with the steepest section climbing above the creek within the first 0.25 mile. The creek is a steady companion, its gurgling not quite loud enough to mask the road noise, but the thick growth along its banks harbors a wealth of birdcall and shade.

The meadow is the high point both in altitude and sensory satisfaction. Be prepared for insect assaults and soggy stretches if you visit in late spring and early summer; a camera and binoculars will help you spot and retain images of the birds and flowers you're likely to see.

The nature trail takes a sharp turn at its head and begins a downhill run, sandwiched between Northwoods Boulevard and the creek. Along sections of this stretch, the path doubles as a rustic neighborhood sidewalk, then hugs the wall of the creek drainage before closing the loop and returning to the clubhouse and trailhead.

Miles and Directions

0.0 Start by crossing Northwoods Boulevard to the signed nature trail on the west side of the road.

0.1 Arrive at the fork at the beginning of the loop; stay left (west), traveling in a clockwise direction. Houses are visible through the lodgepole pines on the left (west).

0.2 The trail begins a short, rocky, attention-demanding climb.

0.4 A social trail from the adjacent neighborhood comes in from the left (southwest). Stay straight (right/west) on the nature trail.

0.5 Cross the first boardwalk at the beaver dam; the valley widens with the trail skirting the west side of the meadow.

0.8 At the junction with the trail to Baden Road, go right (north) on the nature trail.

1.1 Cross the creek and pass a bench before arriving at the junction at the head of the nature loop. Go sharply right

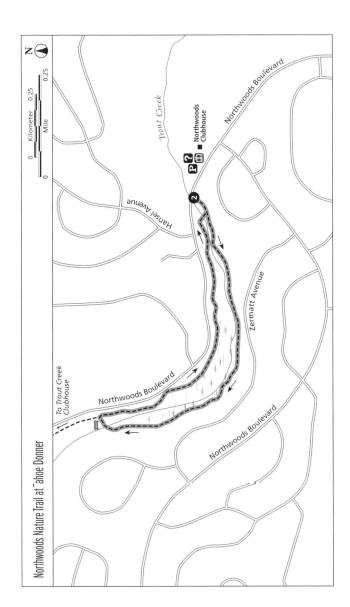

Northwoods Nature Trail at Tahoe Donner

N

Kilometer 0   0.25

Mile 0   0.25

Trout Creek

Hansel Avenue

P ?

ⓘ ■ Northwoods
Clubhouse

2

Zermatt Avenue

Northwoods Boulevard

Northwoods Boulevard

Northwoods Boulevard

To Trout Creek
Clubhouse

(south) on the signed nature trail; the left-hand trail heads north to the Trout Creek clubhouse.

1.5 The doubletrack steepens as it leaves the meadow and descends along the creek drainage.

2.0 Close the loop at the trail fork.

2.1 Arrive back at the trailhead.

Options: A network of multiuse trails offers a variety of opportunities for exploration in the western reaches of Tahoe Donner. Many follow fire roads and offer great views of Donner Lake and the Truckee River valley. Pick up or download a trail map and explore.

3 Martis Creek Wildlife Area

In the biggest expanse of meadow and marshland in the Tahoe area, wildlife thrives. The birds dominate, chirping, flitting, and soaring over the landscape. But whether you love birds or not, an exploration of the enormous grassland surrounding Martis Creek in Martis Valley provides a heavenly hiking experience.

Distance: 4.2-mile loop
Approximate hiking time: 2.5 hours
Difficulty: Moderate due only to length
Trail surface: Dirt singletrack; boardwalk
Best seasons: Late spring, summer, fall
Other trail users: Trail runners, mountain bikers on the Tomkins Memorial Trail (not permitted on the Martis Creek Trail)
Canine compatibility: Leashed dogs permitted on the Tomkins Memorial Trail. Please pick up after your pet; bags are provided at the trailhead. Do not leave bags along the trail.
Fees and permits: None
Schedule: Sunrise to sunset daily
Maps: USGS Martis Peak and Truckee (CA); maps are also posted at the trailhead and along the route. Interpretive signs at the trailhead are also informative.
Trail contact: U.S. Army Corps of Engineers, P.O. Box 2344, Truckee, CA 96161; (530) 587-8113; http://corpslakes.usace .army.mil/visitors/martiscreek
Special considerations: Avoid the fragile Martis Creek Trail if possible, which has been damaged by overuse.

The trail passes through an important heritage area for the native Washoe Indians. Removal of artifacts or damaging historic or prehistoric sites is prohibited by law.

The Army Corps of Engineers, which oversees the trail, also maintains a wonderful campground across CA 267, north of the wildlife area.

Finding the trailhead: From the signalized junction of CA 28 and CA 267 in Kings Beach, follow CA 267 for 8.3 miles, over Brockway summit, to the signed Martis Creek Wildlife Area turnoff on the left (south). Follow the gravel access road for 0.1 mile to the trailhead. From I-80 in Truckee, take exit 188b and head south for 3 miles, past the main entrance for Martis Creek Lake, to the trailhead access road on the right. Parking is limited; if spaces are full, park along the access road or visit another day. Trailhead amenities include an informational kiosk with maps and picnic facilities. GPS: N39 18.096' / W120 07.840'

The Hike

Willow-lined Martis Creek winds a clean, sinuous path through acres and acres of wetland meadow. The creek cuts deep into the turf and branches through the grasses, watering a springtime bloom of wildflowers and providing sustenance for a variety of creatures.

The birds are most prominent, their songs loud enough to be heard over the hum and purr of cars passing on the nearby highway. Songbirds flit from willow to rose to thatch of grass in flashes of brown, black, red, yellow, and sometimes vivid blue; watch for raptors stilling in the clear mountain air and swallows shooting in and out of the highway underpass. Fish, amphibians, and mammals large and small also call the wildlife area home.

The Tomkins Memorial Trail arcs through the sanctuary in a long loop that first immerses hikers in the meadow ecosystem, then in the neighboring forest that cloaks the slopes of the Lookout Peak, Northstar's ski area. The hospitable meadowland has known human habitation for 10,000 years or more, so you'll never be far from signs of civilization, be it the golf course, private homes, or the occasional airplane approaching or leaving the regional airport.

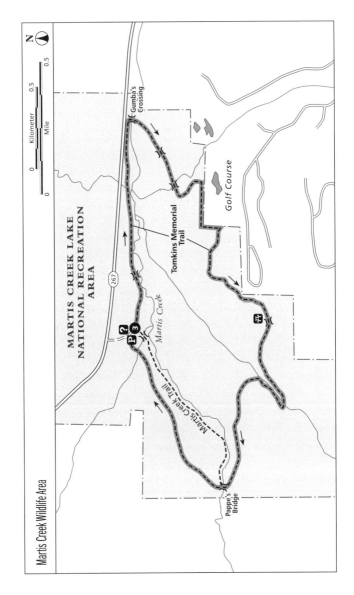

Martis Creek Wildlife Area

MARTIS CREEK LAKE
NATIONAL RECREATION
AREA

267

Gumba's
Crossing

Tomkins Memorial
Trail

Golf Course

Martis Creek

Martis Creek Trail

Pappe's
Bridge

P ?
3

N

Kilometer   0   0.5
Mile   0   0.5

The Tomkins Memorial Trail loop is described clockwise. The trail parallels the highway at the outset, following a broad track easily shared with other trail users. At one of many named bridges spanning the wandering creek and its tributaries, the trail breaks south toward Northstar, traversing sometimes soggy meadow via boardwalks and singletrack.

The metal roofs of Northstar's private homes glint through the trees as you approach the base of the mountain. The trail curves west along the edge of the golf course, then through the forest at the bottom of the ski area. A brief foray into the woodland ends back in the meadow, where the Tomkins Memorial Trail hitches up with the Martis Creek Trail.

The track along Martis Creek has been, according to its advocates, nearly loved into oblivion. The onetime cattle path is the subject of rehabilitation efforts, with temporary fences restricting access to its eroding, willow-choked banks. It's best to finish the meadow tour on the Tomkins Trail, using a boardwalk and well-maintained track to circle back to the trailhead. A bench along this final stretch offers hikers a chance to rest and look down across the creek and valley. The Tomkins Trail meets the Martis Creek path below the parking area; a short easy climb leads out of the bottomlands and back to the trailhead.

Miles and Directions

0.0 Start on the signed Tomkins Memorial Trail, following the broad path that parallels the highway.

0.5 Cross Frank's Fish Bridge, the first of many named spans.

0.8 Reach Gumba's Crossing. Cross the bridge then head southeast across the boardwalk.

1.0 Cross the Green Team's Bridge, then the Broken Bridge.

1.4 Pass under power lines and curl north as the trail runs along the fenced boundary between the wildlife area and the golf course.

1.6 At a break in the fence, marked by a trail sign, go right (northwest) to continue the loop. The left-hand path leads up into the neighborhood.

1.9 Pass a picnic table shaded by massive twin Jeffrey pines, then cross Michael Cousin's Bridge.

2.2 Now in the woodland, pass several junctions with social trails leading back into the neighborhood. Stay right (southwest) at the junctions on the obvious Tomkins Memorial Trail.

2.6 A picnic table and trail map at the edge of a small meadow mark a sharp turn in the trail.

2.9 Reach a bench at the interface between meadow and woodland.

3.1 Pass through scrubland to another trail sign. Ignore side trails, staying straight (west) on the broad main track.

3.3 Arrive at Pappe's Bridge, with a picnic table and a trail sign. The Tomkins Memorial Trail continues straight (west) via a boardwalk; continue on this track. The signed Martis Creek Trail breaks to the right (north).

4.1 Meet the Martis Creek Trail below the trailhead and climb toward the parking area.

4.2 Arrive back at the trailhead.

4 Tahoe Meadows Interpretive Trail

Meandering through a lovely meadow beneath the summits of Slide Mountain and Mount Rose, this flat, friendly interpretive route is perfect for families, wildflower enthusiasts, view seekers, and those looking for an alpine experience with little sweat involved.

Distance: 1.3-mile loop
Approximate hiking time: 1 hour
Difficulty: Easy
Trail surface: Dirt singletrack; bridges
Best seasons: Summer and fall
Other trail users: None
Canine compatibility: Leashed dogs permitted
Fees and permits: None
Schedule: Sunrise to sunset daily
Maps: USGS Mount Rose (NV); Tom Harrison Recreation Map of Lake Tahoe
Trail contact: USDA Forest Service, Lake Tahoe Basin Management Unit, Forest Supervisor's Office, 35 College Dr., South Lake Tahoe, CA 96150; (530) 543-2600; www.fs.fed.us/r5/ltbmu. Tahoe Rim Trail Association, 948 Incline Way, Incline Village, NV 89451; (775) 298-0233; www.tahoerimtrail.org
Other: This was formerly known as the Tahoe Meadows Whole Access Trail. The route is wheelchair and stroller accessible for the first 0.5 mile. There is a large restroom at the trailhead.

Finding the trailhead: From the intersection of NV 28 and Village Boulevard in Incline Village, head west on NV 28 to NV 431 (the scenic Mount Rose Highway). Go right (northeast) onto NV 431 for 7.3 miles to the signed trailhead on the right (east). From Tahoe City follow CA 28 (which becomes NV 28 once you cross the state line in Crystal Bay) for 14 miles to the junction with NV 431. Turn left (north) and follow NV 431 to the trailhead parking area. Information signs are at the trailhead. If no parking is available in the lot, park in the pullout on NV 431. GPS: N39 18.433' / W119 54.436'

Tahoe Meadows Interpretive Trail

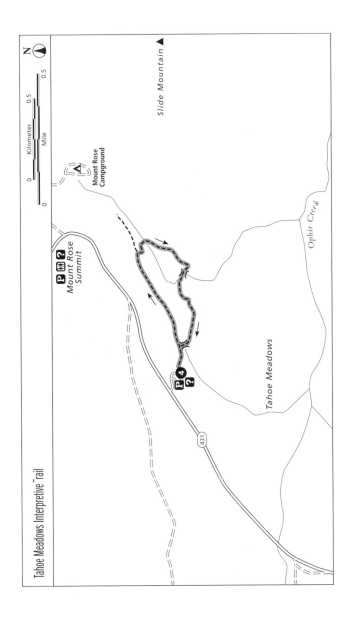

The Hike

Easy and scenic, the Tahoe Meadows loop skirts a verdant swath of grass and wildflowers at nearly 8,700 feet, offering access to stands of stately evergreens, a chance to study a habitat that spends much of the year under a thick blanket of snow, and vistas of high ridges that stretch south to Lake Tahoe and up to the stony summits of Slide Mountain and Mount Rose.

The first part of the trail is accessible to hardy wheelchair users, and a family with small children, whether in a stroller, in a backpack, or toddling, can manage the entire loop. Though the Mount Rose Highway, a lovely and popular drive, is never distant, the scenery more than qualifies this as an alpine experience.

A trail sign behind the restroom marks the hike's start. Follow the well-groomed dirt path into the meadow; at an interpretive sign and boardwalk/bridge, the trail splits, forming a loop. Stay left (north), as the signs indicate, traveling the loop in a clockwise direction.

Though the trail, part of the Tahoe Rim Trail, is gently climbing at the outset, it's never strenuous. The path merges into a patch of pavement, then reverts to natural surface as it traces the edge of the meadow. Altitude-stunted evergreens briefly block the meadow views, then the route traces the interface of forest and meadow as it approaches the head of the meadow.

Diverge from the Tahoe Rim Trail, which continues northeast toward Mount Rose, at a trail sign. Stay right (east) on the nature trail, curving south toward the Lake Tahoe basin and walking through mature woodland. Interpretive signs along this stretch describe frogs and fish, butterflies and birds, human habitation and hibernation. Bridges span the stream that waters the meadow, and you can spot the tiny fish that somehow survive at these heights.

The trail emerges from the forest to cross small bridges and boardwalks in the moist meadow. Views down the mountain open into a blue void: the Tahoe basin with the lake 2,000 feet below and out of sight. Close the loop at the bridge and trail sign, then retrace your steps back to the trailhead.

Miles and Directions

0.0 Start at the information sign.

0.1 The trail splits at an interpretive sign and bridge; take the left leg as directed by the trail sign, traveling in a clockwise direction.

0.5 Reach the intersection with the Tahoe Rim Trail, which continues northeast toward Mount Rose. Go right (east) on the interpretive trail.

0.8 Pass a trail marker and cross a bridge over the stream.

1.2 Arrive back at the trail junction to close the loop.

1.3 Arrive back at the trailhead.

5 Incline Village Exercise Course

A trickling stream is the centerpiece of this forested loop just off the beach and close to shopping and lodging. Frequented by dog walkers, trail runners, and families, the exercise stations seem an afterthought—except for those looking to firm up as well as mellow out.

Distance: 1.1-mile loop
Approximate hiking time: 45 minutes to 1 hour
Difficulty: Easy
Trail surface: Dirt singletrack
Best seasons: Late spring, summer, fall
Other trail users: Dog walkers, fitness buffs
Canine compatibility: Leashed dogs permitted (but also run off-leash)

Fees and permits: None
Schedule: Sunrise to sunset daily
Maps: USGS Marlette Lake (NV), but no map is needed
Trail contact: Incline Village General Improvement District, Parks and Recreation Department; 980 Incline Way, Incline Village, NV 89451; (775) 832-1300; www.ivgid.org or www.inclinerecreation.com

Finding the trailhead: From the signalized junction of Village Boulevard and NV 28 in Incline Village, follow Village Boulevard south (toward the lake) for 0.6 mile to Lakeshore Boulevard. Go left (east) onto Lakeshore Boulevard for 0.1 mile to the Aspen Grove parking lot opposite Ski Beach. The signed trailhead is just inside the parking lot entrance on the left. A parking attendant may be on duty on busy summer days. A generous parking lot and restrooms are available, and the Aspen Grove Community Center and Village Green are nearby. GPS: N39 14.312' / W119 56.523'

The Hike

The mulching duff on the forest floor surrounding this short trail yields striking eruptions of brilliant red snow plant in late spring and early summer. You can't miss them—the conical flower stalks quite literally glow when caught in the sun, and once you spot one, you'll see them everywhere.

Snow plant is relatively common in the lower montane forests surrounding Lake Tahoe. The red color indicates the plants have no chlorophyll, instead gleaning nutrition from rotting plants on the forest floor and from a parasitic relationship with a fungus in the roots systems of pines. Its scientific name, according to the USDA Forest Service's Rangeland Management Botany Program Web site, translates to "the bloody flesh-like thing." An accurate, if gory, description.

The trail winds through a moderately urban—and very urbane—setting. With the green bulk of the Hyatt Regency rising above the grassy expanse of the Village Green on the east side of the trail and wood-sided housing on the west, the route navigates through a strip of forest watered by two streams and dotted with numbered exercise stations. The path, which was upgraded in 2009 including stream rehabilitation, is popular with joggers and dog walkers who sometimes let their pooches off leashes to frolic in the water.

Begin at the signed trailhead just inside the Aspen Grove parking lot. Drop across the creek on parallel boards; the trail splits on the other side, forming a loop. Stay right (north and streamside), following the route in a counterclockwise direction. The exercise stations, with structures designed to help build strength and flexibility, along with trail signs, help keep you on track.

The forest is open enough to allow views of the Village

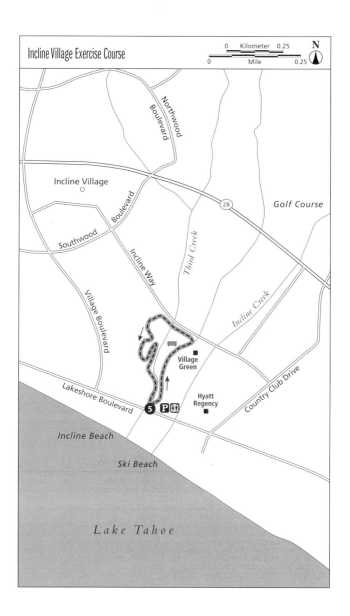

Incline Village Exercise Course

Lake Tahoe

Green, the Hyatt, and the high peaks above the town. Just beyond a trail junction and a seat carved in a fallen tree on the left (west), the loop bumps up against Incline Way and curves westward past a couple of exercise stops, then crosses a second stream and heads back south toward the lake. Though social trails merge in this area, signs mark the route. And there's no way to get lost—the Village Green and neighborhood houses define the boundaries of the greenbelt.

At a parking area the trail curves back on itself, heading north for a short distance before curling south again past more exercise stations. Bob and weave through the rest of the signs and stops, following the arrows, to close the loop near the stream. Unless you want to do laps, cross the creek to return to the trailhead.

Miles and Directions

0.0 Start at the signed trailhead, crossing the creek and staying right (north) where the trail splits.

0.3 Pass a seat carved in a fallen log.

0.4 The trail meets Incline Way. Social trails converge as the path arcs left (west) toward a second stream and a gated roadway. Cross the stream and follow the track wedged between the waterway and the road. Continue south (toward Lake Tahoe) on the signed path.

0.7 Reach the parking lot and curl back north to cross the stream. Close the loop, then cross back over the creek.

1.1 Arrive back at the trailhead.

Options: A network of walking trails follows Lakeshore Drive and winds through the neighborhoods of Incline Village. Mostly paved, these paths connect businesses, schools, and recreation sites throughout the village.

6 Sand Point Nature Trail

Take a break from the sun and water with a quick stroll along the boardwalk at Sand Point. With views across Lake Tahoe and into rocky coves along the shoreline, and interpretive signs describing some of the components that make the lake's environment so beautiful and unique, the loop is perfect for families.

Distance: 0.4-mile loop
Approximate hiking time: 30 minutes
Difficulty: Easy
Trail surface: Boardwalk; brick walkway
Best seasons: Year-round
Other trail users: None
Canine compatibility: Dogs not permitted
Fees and permits: Day-use fee
Schedule: The park is open from 8:00 a.m. to 9:00 p.m. from Memorial Day to Labor Day. From May 1 to Memorial Day, and from Labor Day to September 30, hours are from 8:00 a.m. to 7:00 p.m. From October 1 to April 30 hours are from 8:00 a.m. to 5:00 p.m.
Maps: USGS Marlette Lake (NV), but no map is needed
Trail contact: Lake Tahoe–Nevada State Park, P.O. Box 8867, Incline Village, NV 89452; (775) 831-0494; parks.nv.gov/lt.htm
Other: Sand Harbor features swimming, boating, picnic facilities, and a visitor center and gift shop. The park also hosts the annual Lake Tahoe Shakespeare Festival in July and August; the amphitheater is cupped inside the trail loop.
Special considerations: The trail is wheelchair accessible.

Finding the trailhead: From the junction of NV 28 and Village Boulevard in Incline Village, follow NV 28 south along Lake Tahoe's east shore for 4.8 miles to the signed park entrance on the right (west). The parking lots fill by midmorning on summer days,

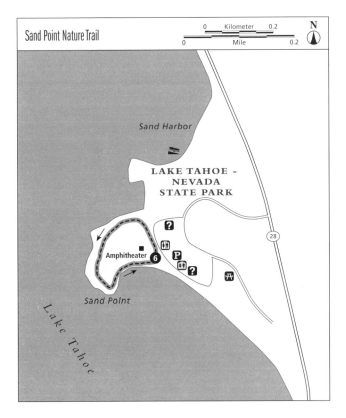

Sand Point Nature Trail

restricting access to the park and trail. Parking, water, restrooms, and a visitor center and gift shop are near the trailhead. GPS: N39 11.849' / W119 55.886'

The Hike

Visit Sand Harbor early in the day and you'll find the usually busy beach nearly deserted, though the parking lot may bustle with divers preparing to explore Sand Harbor and Lake Tahoe. You'll also likely have the boardwalk that circles Sand Point all to yourself, a rare treat sweetened with amazing vistas. On a typical summer morning, the smooth lake surface reflects a sky of uninterrupted blue, and the low sun casts defining shadows on rock formations cluttering the shoreline.

But don't wait for morning to visit the trail—it's delightful at any time of day. Super easy, wheelchair and stroller accessible, and lined with interpretive signs, the route is a fine addition to any East Shore visit.

Begin on the north side of the restrooms at an informational kiosk, stepping onto an elevated walkway constructed of recycled plastic boards. The boardwalk overlooks a small rocky cove where divers enter the cold water and kayakers launch. Ponderosa pines, snow fences, interpretive signs, and jumbles of granite line the route.

As you round Sand Point (traveling counterclockwise), the trail surface changes to brick, and short side trails lead to vista points overlooking tiny coves guarded by granite boulders. The last section of the trail looks down on the huge sandy beach, often thickly blanketed with sunbathers and colorful shade umbrellas. The trail ends in front of the restrooms near the entrance to the amphitheater.

Miles and Directions

0.0   Start at the kiosk on the north side of the restrooms.

0.2   Short side trails lead to vista points. Explore the shoreline, returning to the main trail and continuing the circuit.

0.4   Arrive back at the trailhead.

Option: A 0.6-mile trail along Lake Tahoe's shoreline links Sand Harbor to Memorial Point, where you'll find more interpretive signage, restrooms, parking, and short paths that lead to overlooks.

7 Skunk Harbor

Skunk Harbor is no stinker. A broad, steep track leads down to a secluded bay where the clear water of Lake Tahoe washes in a rainbow arc onto the stone-strewn beach, melting from indigo to turquoise to gold as it approaches the shore. An "upside down" hike, with the climb on the return trip, you can prepare for the ascent by enjoying lunch and resting in the front yard of the old Newhall House.

Distance: 3 miles out and back
Approximate hiking time: 2 hours
Difficulty: Moderate due to an elevation change of more than 600 feet
Trail surface: Dirt access road
Best seasons: Late spring, summer, fall
Other trail users: The occasional hardy mountain biker
Canine compatibility: Leashed dogs permitted
Fees and permits: None
Schedule: Sunrise to sunset daily

Maps: USGS Marlette Lake (NV); Lake Tahoe Basin Management Unit Map; Tom Harrison Recreation Map of Lake Tahoe
Trail contact: USDA Forest Service Lake Tahoe Basin Management Unit, Forest Supervisor's Office, 35 College Dr., South Lake Tahoe, CA 96150; (530) 543-2600; www.fs.fed.us/r5/ltbmu
Other: Limited parking and the lack of signage make the trailhead a challenge to find but ensure that the route will not be crowded.

Finding the trailhead: From the junction of NV 28 and Village Boulevard in Incline Village, follow NV 28 south along the east shore for 9.3 miles to the unsigned trailhead on the right (west/lakeside). From the intersection of US 50 and CA 89 in South Lake Tahoe, drive 17.9 miles north on US 50 to its intersection with NV 28 near Spooner Summit. Turn left (north) onto NV 28 and go about 2.4

miles to the trailhead, which is on the left side of the highway. A green gate tucked below the highway blocks vehicle access to the trail. There is parking for about five cars along the highway above the gate, and ten to twelve spaces about 100 yards up (north) of the trailhead in a pullout. No other amenities are available. GPS: N39 07.717' / W119 55.888'

The Hike

As if the sandy beach, sun-baked rocks, and cool, clear water weren't enough to draw hikers down to lakeside, Skunk Harbor is also the site of the picturesque Newhall House, built in 1923 as a wedding gift from George Newhall to his wife, Caroline. A plaque explains the origin and preservation of the house, but the true monument is the rustic structure itself, all stonework and peaked roofs and heavy wooden window frames. Peek through barred windows into the gloomy interior, then spread a picnic on one of the verandas, enjoying the wonderful views.

Swimming and picnicking are popular activities for all who venture down the steep access road to the harbor. Powerboats sometimes drop anchor in the cove, sharing the scene with those on foot. But even with some coming by land and others by water, the destination is seldom crowded.

To begin, pass the gate and head down on the paved, then dirt, roadway. The old roadway flattens and circles through a drainage, then traverses the mountainside. From the traverse you can catch views of Slaughterhouse Canyon and the lake beyond.

When you reach the unsigned trail fork with the road into Slaughterhouse Canyon, stay right (straight) on the broad road to Skunk Harbor. The route drops more steeply,

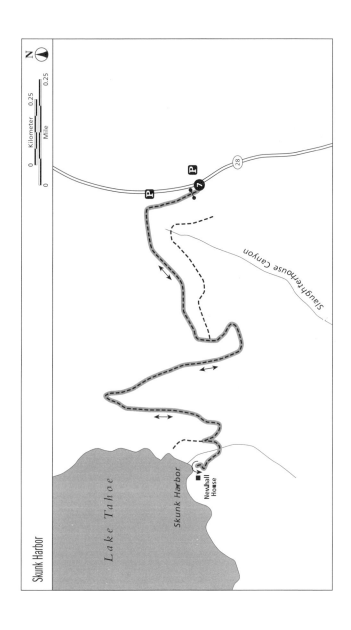

Skunk Harbor

Lake Tahoe

Skunk Harbor

Newhall House

Slaughterhouse Canyon

28

N

Kilometer
0   0.25

Mile
0   0.25

rounding a switchback and passing through a clearing. Another switchback loops through woodland, then the trail narrows and enters a swampy area watered by an ephemeral stream.

Just beyond the moist patch, the trail forks. Go left (west), and meander down through lush undergrowth, crossing a streamlet, to the Newhall House. Footpaths lead around to the lake side of the house and Skunk Harbor proper, with a ruined dock stretching into the water. Explore the beach then return as you came, keeping in mind that it's all uphill from the bay. It takes a bit longer to climb out than it does to descend.

Miles and Directions

0.0 Start by passing the green gate and heading down the broad access road.

0.4 Pass the junction with the trail that leads left (down and south) to Slaughterhouse Canyon. Stay right (down and west) on the road to Skunk Harbor.

1.0 Round a switchback.

1.4 Reach the T junction above the harbor. Beach access trails are to the right (north); the house is to the left (south).

1.5 Arrive at the house and beach. Rest and relax at the waterside, then retrace your steps.

3.0 Arrive back at the trailhead.

8 Spooner Lake Loop

Once a water source for miners working silver mines near Virginia City, Spooner Lake supplies hikers with a splendid short hike that circumnavigates its forested shoreline.

Distance: 2.1-mile loop

Approximate hiking time: 1.5 hours

Difficulty: Easy

Trail surface: Singletrack; dirt roadway; pavement

Best seasons: Late spring, summer, fall (when the aspens turn)

Other trail users: None on the loop itself; cyclists on the portions leading to and from the loop

Canine compatibility: Leashed dogs permitted

Fees and permits: Day-use fee

Schedule: The park is open from 8:00 a.m. to 9:00 p.m. from Memorial Day to Labor Day. From May 1 to Memorial Day, and from Labor Day to September 30, hours are from 8:00 a.m. to 7:00 p.m. From October 1 to April 30, hours are from 8:00 a.m. to 5:00 p.m.

Maps: USGS Glenbrook (NV); state park map available at the entrance station; information board map at the trailhead

Trail contact: Lake Tahoe–Nevada State Park, P.O. Box 8867, Incline Village, NV 89452; (775) 831-0494; parks.nv.gov/lt.htm

Finding the trailhead: From the junction of NV 28 and Village Boulevard in Incline Village, follow NV 28 south for about 11 miles to the signed turnoff into Lake Tahoe–Nevada State Park. Turn left (east) into the park and follow the park road to the trailhead. From South Lake Tahoe/Stateline, follow US 50 north for about 12 miles to the junction with NV 28. Go left (west) onto NV 28 for 0.5 mile to the park entrance on the right. Parking is available, plus restrooms, water, information, and picnic areas. GPS: N39 06.369' / W119 54.963'

The Hike

Glades of quaking aspen, their chattering leaves bright green in spring and vivid gold in fall, crowd the first mile of this flat, easy circuit around Spooner Lake. The aspen groves, some featuring gnarly old specimens with thick trunks scarred by graffiti, blend into an evergreen woodland on the lake's northern shores, with wildflowers sprinkled in meadow grasses flourishing in small clearings. Breaks in the trees allow views to open across the water, where ducks and other waterfowl are virtually guaranteed to be swimming and spotting an osprey is possible.

The large information sign at the trailhead—the first of a series of interpretive signs scattered along the loop—shows the extensive trail system that explores the Marlette Lake–Hobart Reservoir backcountry. Spooner Lake offers a sampling of what you'd find farther in.

Interpretive signs also detail how the lake was integrated into the complex water and lumber delivery systems that fed resources from the Sierra to the silver mines on Nevada's high desert. An amazing array of railroads, haul roads, and flumes (one 17 miles long) originating around Lake Tahoe carried water and timber to the mines, with Spooner Lake, then part of Spooner Ranch, strategically located near the east side summit. The ranch owner, Michel Spooner, along with a partner, established Spooner Station in 1860, with a mill, hotel, saloon, and more accommodating the needs of miners, lumberjacks, and travelers.

From the trailhead follow the signed paved path down through a boulder-bordered picnic area (where interpretive signs detail the history of the lake, the wildlife and plant life it supports, and cross-country skiing opportunities) to the lakeshore trail. The loop begins here and is described in a counterclockwise direction.

The ecotones—meadow, aspen forest, evergreen forest—merge seamlessly as you follow the well-maintained singletrack, dotted with viewing benches, around the lake. Highway noise from US 50 can be a distraction at the outset, but it fades as you reach the woods on the northern shoreline, and trees screen it from view.

Near the halfway point you'll reach the junction with the Tahoe Rim Trail; follow a section of the TRT back to the lake's earthen dam. Most of the anglers hang out at the dam, with rocky beaches suitable for picnicking just north of the structure. The bugs can be brutal here; walk with your mouth closed!

The dam is also where the loop closes. From the trail junction climb up through the woods to the parking area and trailhead.

Miles and Directions

0.0 Start at the trailhead next to the restrooms, signed for ALL TRAILS. Follow the paved path to the large information sign, where you'll stay right (east) to Spooner Lake. Pass through the split-rail fence and stay left (northeast) to a picnic area surrounded by boulders.

0.1 Follow the dirt path down to a gravel road. Turn right (south); in 25 yards the signed Spooner Lake Loop breaks left (east) and heads down into a meadow.

0.6 Stay left (straight) on the Spooner Lake Loop, where an access trail breaks right toward the highway, and drop into quaking aspen groves.

1.0 Cross a boardwalk over the inlet stream and climb to the junction with the Tahoe Rim Trail. Go left (southwest) on the signed TRT/Spooner Lake Loop.

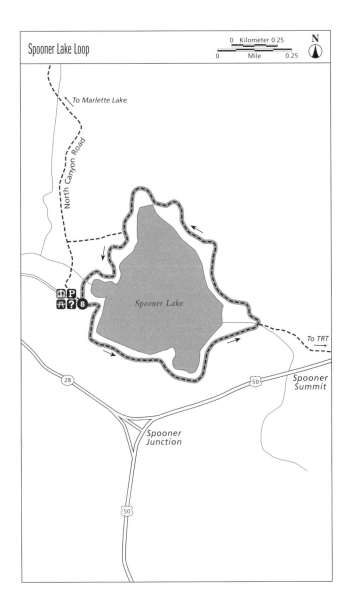

Spooner Lake Loop

0   Kilometer   0.25

0   Mile   0.25

N

To Marlette Lake

North Canyon Road

Spooner Lake

To TRT

Spooner Summit

Spooner Junction

28

50

50

1.6 At the junction with the link to the North Canyon Road to Marlette Lake, stay left (south), following the shoreline.

1.8 Arrive at the dam and a trail junction. Cross the dam and go down through the spillway. Pass a signboard listing angling regulations, then cross the gravel road to the sign that points uphill to the parking area. Two paths lead through the woods; pick one and start the short climb.

2.1 Arrive back at the trailhead.

Options: Miles of trails head north into the Marlette-Hobart backcountry from the Spooner Lake trailhead. The Tahoe Rim Trail can be reached from the nearby Spooner Summit trailhead, located a short distance up NV 28 and US 50 from the park entrance. From the summit the TRT heads north to Snow Valley Peak, Marlette Lake, and beyond; heading south, it skirts Duane Bliss Peak and continues to the Kingsbury Grade. The famous Flume Trail, a mountain biker's favorite, and the road to Marlette Lake, an easy hike save for its distance, are excellent options for the more experienced hiker.

9 Five Lakes Trail

Summertime views of a ski area can be shocking—slopes traversed easily when covered with snow look much steeper when their bare rock underpinnings are revealed. The climb to Five Lakes offers access (not lift-served) to the slopes near Alpine Meadows, then mellows in the shady forest surrounding the lakes themselves.

Distance: 4.2 miles out and back
Approximate hiking time: 2 hours
Trail surface: Dirt singletrack
Difficulty: More challenging due to 1,000-foot elevation gain. The trail is mostly shadeless and can be hot.
Best seasons: Late spring, summer mornings, fall
Other trail users: None
Canine compatibility: Dogs permitted except where posted in the Granite Chief Wilderness
Fees and permits: None
Schedule: Sunrise to sunset daily
Maps: USGS Tahoe City and Granite Chief (CA); Lake Tahoe Basin Management Unit Map
Trail contact: USDA Forest Service Tahoe National Forest, 9646 Donner Pass Rd., Truckee, CA 96161; (530) 587-3558; www .fs.fed.us/r5/tahoe. USDA Forest Service Lake Tahoe Basin Management Unit, Forest Supervisor's Office, 35 College Dr., South Lake Tahoe, CA 96150; (530) 543-2600; www.fs.fed.us/r5/ ltbmu
Special considerations: Given the elevation gain and exposure to the elements, do not attempt the hike if you have heart, respiratory, or knee problems.

Finding the trailhead: From the intersection of CA 89 and CA 28 in Tahoe City, follow CA 89 northwest (toward Truckee) for 3.6 miles. Turn left (west) onto Alpine Meadows Road and go 2.2 miles to the trailhead, which is across from the second intersection with

Deer Park Drive. Limited parking is available along Alpine Meadows Road; no other amenities are available. GPS: N39 10.749' / W120 13.790'

The Hike

Three distinct settings, and thus three distinct moods, lie along the trail to Five Lakes. The most arduous part of the trek is at the outset, where switchbacks climb through a sun-fed thicket of manzanita, mule ear, and snowberry. The second section features great views of the Alpine Meadows Ski Area, metal ski lift towers punched into smooth, colorful granite slabs, and an exposed traverse of a shallow granite-walled canyon. On the short third leg, a thick fir forest takes over, obscuring views and hiding all but one of the five small lakes that nestle within its confines.

As for the moods—well, the first pitch is vexing; the second pitch, amid the granite and towers, boasts the best views; and the third is peaceful and contemplative. Enjoy!

Begin by climbing switchbacks on the hillside north of Bear Creek. Switchbacks, switchbacks, and more switchbacks—keep climbing until you leave the scrub behind. Now very alpine in feel, you can look down-canyon from the trail toward the Truckee River valley and up-canyon onto the slopes of the Alpine Meadows Ski Area.

Traverse to yet another switchback, then climb under ski lift towers into a saddle, where the trail enters a narrowing side canyon with black-streaked walls. Two switchbacks are built like giant stair steps into orange rock; beyond, the trail traverses above the shallowing canyon to more gentle switchbacks. At the outskirts of the fir forest, a sign denotes the boundary of the Granite Chief Wilderness.

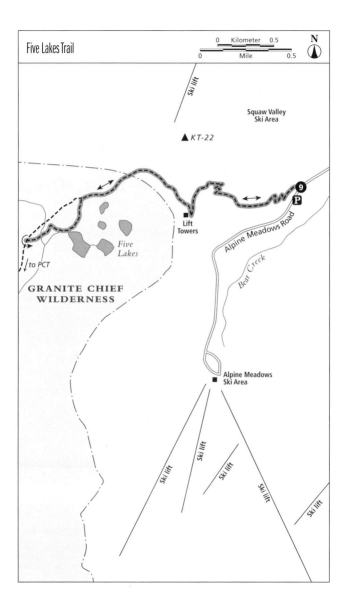

Five Lakes Trail

0   Kilometer   0.5

0   Mile   0.5

N

Ski lift

Squaw Valley
Ski Area

▲ KT-22

Ski lift

Lift
Towers

Alpine Meadows Road

Bear Creek

Five
Lakes

to PCT

GRANITE CHIEF
WILDERNESS

9

P

Alpine Meadows
Ski Area

Ski lift

Ski lift

Ski lift

Ski lift

Ski lift

Trails collide in the woods. At the signed junction with the Pacific Crest Trail (PCT), go left (south) to the shoreline of one of the small lakes, where social trails lead to inviting rest spots on the water. You'll have to bushwhack and do some clever off-trail navigating to find the other, nearby lakes. Visit for a time, then return as you came.

Miles and Directions

0.0 Start at the GRANITE CHIEF WILDERNESS trail sign. It's all uphill from here, with switchbacks and granite stair steps aiding in the climb. Take it slow and enjoy the views.

1.1 Pass under several ski area lift towers (you'll want a chair by this point!).

1.2 Cross a small saddle and curve into a granite-walled side canyon, passing a trail marker and a private property sign.

1.4 Negotiate switchbacks carved into orange rock.

1.7 Pass the GRANITE CHIEF WILDERNESS sign.

2.0 At the signed junction of the Five Lakes Trail and the PCT to Whiskey Creek Camp, stay left (south).

2.1 Reach the shoreline of one of the Five Lakes. The others can't be seen. This is the turnaround point.

4.2 Arrive back at the trailhead.

Option: The trail continues through a meadow and on to a second junction with the PCT at 2.5 miles. From there you can hike or backpack to Whiskey Creek Camp and other destinations in the Granite Chief Wilderness.

10 Truckee River Trail

One of the easiest and most popular trails in north Lake Tahoe, this well-maintained paved route traces the Truckee River from Tahoe City to Alpine Meadows Road and beyond. Along the way you'll enjoy views of the sparkling river, the lush riparian habitat that lines its banks, the dark evergreen forest that blankets the valley walls, and the crowds that float the river and enjoy the trail with you.

Distance: 7.2 miles out and back
Approximate hiking time: 4 hours
Difficulty: Moderate due only to length
Trail surface: Paved bike path
Best seasons: Spring, summer, fall
Other trail users: Lots of cyclists, in-line skaters, runners
Canine compatibility: Leashed dogs permitted
Fees and permits: None

Schedule: Sunrise to sunset daily
Maps: USGS Tahoe City (CA); Lake Tahoe Basin Management Unit Map; Tom Harrison Recreation Map of Lake Tahoe
Trail contact: Tahoe City Public Utility District, Parks and Recreation Department, P.O. Box 5249, Tahoe City, CA 96145; (530) 583-3440 ext. 10; www.tcpud.org
Special considerations: The route is wheelchair accessible.

Finding the trailhead: From the signalized intersection of CA 89 and CA 28 in Tahoe City, go 0.2 mile south on CA 89 to a signed right turn into the large trailhead parking area at 64 Acre Park. You'll find restrooms and interpretive signage at the trailhead. Porta-pottys are spaced along the trail. GPS: N39 9.877' / W120 8.840'

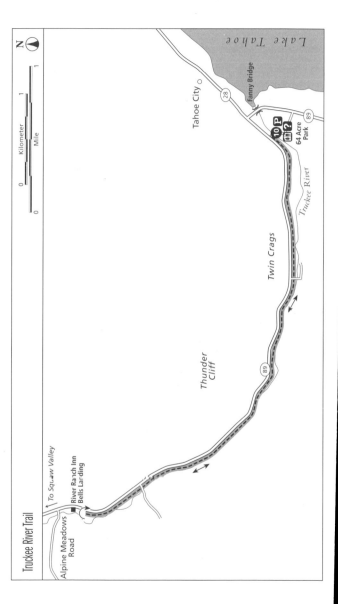

Truckee River Trail

N

Kilometer
0   1

Mile
0   1

Alpine Meadows Road

To Squaw Valley

River Ranch Inn
Bells Landing

Thunder Cliff

89

Twin Crags

Truckee River

Tahoe City

28

Fanny Bridge

89

64 Acre Park

Lake Tahoe

The Hike

On long hot summer days, the Truckee River swirls with the revelry of river rafters. The clear water, reflecting the browns and grays of its rocky bottom, is topped by the dazzling blues, oranges, and yellows of the rafts, and the spectacular colors of boaters' swimsuits and hats. This riotous rainbow spills onto the trail that follows the river from Tahoe City to the inn at River Run, where the neon Lycra of cyclists, runners, and in-line skaters mingles with the pastels worn by babies in strollers.

It is virtually impossible to get lost on the Truckee River Trail; if you wander into the water or find you are sharing pavement with automobiles, you've strayed from the route. Mile markers are also provided. A broken yellow line down the center of the trail separates downstream traffic from those headed upstream. Proximity to the highway precludes any illusion of this being a wilderness hike, but it makes for an entertaining family outing, and it is wheelchair accessible.

The trail begins by crossing the arcing bridge to the north shore of the river, then bears left (west) and runs between the watercourse and CA 89. At the outset pass several businesses and cross a couple of driveways, then drop waterside, where dense willow sometimes hides the meandering river. The only intersections along the trail's length are with the driveways and private bridges of lucky souls whose homes are perched on the riverbanks.

Sandbars in the river offer respite for the rafters; for hikers and other trail users, narrow social paths lead to small rocky or sandy beaches that serve as wonderful viewpoints, picnic spots, or rest and turnaround spots. Hike as far as you'd like; if you have the time and energy, follow the trail all the way to Alpine Meadows Road and River Ranch. Return as you came.

Miles and Directions

0.0   Start by crossing the bridge in 64 Acre Park then turning left (west) onto the paved bike path.

0.2   Cross the access drive for Tahoe City Lumber.

1.0   Pass a mile marker.

2.0   Pass another mile marker and a CONGESTED AREA sign.

3.0   Pass a third mile marker and a private driveway.

3.4   Climb the only hill along the route (it's short) to the rafters' staging area.

3.6   Reach Bells Landing and the inn at River Ranch. Have a cool drink on the patio, then retrace your steps to the trailhead.

7.2   Arrive back at the trailhead.

Options: From River Run you can continue west on the Truckee River Trail to Squaw Valley Road. The total round-trip is 10 miles; maps are available at the parks and recreation department office.

The Truckee River trailhead in Tahoe City also serves as the junction for other lakeshore bike paths, including one that heads north to Dollar Point and one that follows CA 89 south to Sugar Pine Point State Park.

Finally, a nice section of the Tahoe Rim Trail begins near downtown Tahoe City and leads about 2 miles to a vista point. To reach this part of the TRT from near the junction of CA 28 and CA 89, turn right onto Fairway Drive and go 0.2 mile to the parking lot at the Fairway Community Center.

11 Page Meadows

A favorite hike of Tahoe locals and visitors alike, Page Meadows hosts one of the best wildflower blooms in the basin. It greens up by late May, glows with wildflower color by late June, and remains a restful, scenic destination through the rest of the hiking season. A steady climb on the Tahoe Rim Trail leads to the meadows.

Distance: 3.3 miles out and back

Approximate hiking time: 2 hours

Difficulty: Moderate due to length and 400-foot elevation gain

Trail surface: Singletrack and logging road

Best seasons: Late spring and early summer for the wildflower bloom

Other trail users: Mountain bikers, equestrians, off-road vehicles on adjacent trails

Canine compatibility: Dogs permitted

Fees and permits: None

Schedule: Dawn to dusk daily

Maps: USGS Tahoe City (CA); Tahoe Rim Trail map for the Barker Pass to Tahoe City section available at the trailhead and online

Trail contact: USDA Forest Service Lake Tahoe Basin Management Unit, Forest Supervisor's Office, 35 College Dr., South Lake Tahoe, CA 96150; (530) 543-2600; www.fs.fed.us/r5/ltbmu. Tahoe Rim Trail Association, 948 Incline Way, Incline Village, NV 89451; (775) 298-0233; www.tahoerimtrail.org

Finding the trailhead: From Tahoe City follow CA 89 south toward Homewood to Pineland Drive (with large PINELAND signs). Turn right (west) onto Pineland Drive and go 0.3 mile to Twin Peaks Drive, where a sign points you toward WARD VALLEY. Go left (south) onto Twin Peaks, then quickly right (west) onto Ward Creek Boulevard. Follow

Ward Creek Boulevard for 1.5 miles to the signed TRT trailhead. Park alongside Ward Creek Boulevard. No other amenities are available. GPS: N39 08.435' / W120 11.522'

The Hike

High country wildflower displays are colorful but understated, with most flowers blooming modestly in patches that mingle with meadow grasses. Some varieties, like mule ears with their bright yellow sunflower-like flowers and the tall white umbrellas of cow parsnip, border on flamboyance, but most flourish low to the ground, their subtle beauty most vivid upon close inspection.

Page Meadows, situated above the Ward Valley at about 7,000 feet, is the perfect destination for the wildflower lover—or the mountain meadow lover. Rimmed by a thick evergreen forest with a border of aspens that have been sculpted into a low tangle by heavy winter snowpack, a leisurely stroll through the grassland reveals pockets of red Indian paintbrush, purple shooting star, pink pussy paws, and much more early in the season. Later white yarrow and purple and yellow asters (among others) come to the forefront.

The section of the Tahoe Rim Trail that leads from Ward Creek to the meadow begins steeply, with the sound of the creek splashing through its bed a pleasant accompaniment. At about the 0.5-mile mark, the climb mellows and you can pause to take in views of the craggy headwall of Ward Valley, where the architecture of the ridgetops is defined by snow well into June and early July.

Once on the ridgetop the trail is intersected by a number of access and OHV roads and the forest floor is littered with slash, but the route is clearly marked with the distinctive TRT trail markers as well as other signage. Follow the winding trail through the woods until the meadow opens before you.

A narrow path cuts through the thick turf of the meadow, which is wet and even snowy early in the season, with portions under water—shallow vernal pools—into June. Cement landscaping tiles have been laid to delineate the TRT and protect the fragile ecosystem (they also help keep hikers' boots dry), and side trails branch off to explore the meadow. The bugs can be voracious, so wear long sleeves or douse yourself in repellent—otherwise, you may not be able to linger long enough to enjoy the display.

The TRT bridges the main meadow and a smaller meadow through a narrow band of trees, then reenters the forest and rises to a sign noting the distances to the Ward Creek road and Tahoe City. This is the turnaround point. Return as you came to the trailhead.

Miles and Directions

- **0.0** Start on the north side of Ward Creek, where signs mark the singletrack TRT and describe camping regulations.
- **0.1** At the signed junction with a steep dirt roadway, go left (west) and uphill through the woods.
- **0.5** The climb mellows at a bend in the road with views west to the head of Ward Valley.
- **0.7** Climb to a junction marked with an OHV sign. Trail markers for the TRT are about 25 yards ahead, as well as a sign for Page Meadows. Stay left (southwest) on the marked route, crossing two streamlets that may be dry in late season. The route narrows to singletrack.
- **1.1** Reach another trail junction; stay right (northwest) on the signed TRT, passing low posts that prevent motor vehicle access.

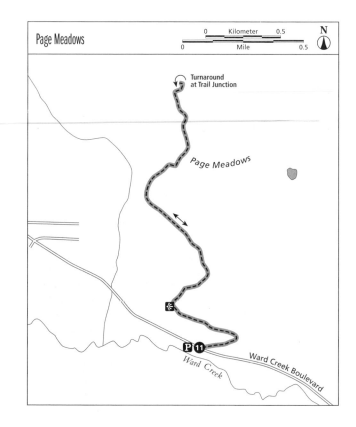

1.2 Arrive at the first (main) meadow.

1.5 Pass through a narrow band of trees to a second, smaller meadow.

1.6 Reach the trail junction with a sign noting distances to the Ward Creek road and Tahoe City. Turn around here and retrace your steps.

3.3 Arrive back at the trailhead.

12 Ellis Peak Trail

Without question this is the toughest hike in this guide, but all the work you'll do climbing onto the ridge above Blackwood Canyon is more than rewarded by the views from the top, where you'll look down onto Lake Tahoe in one direction and onto the granite domes of the Desolation Wilderness in the other. Those with thighs of steel can continue to peaceful Ellis Lake.

Distance: 2 miles out and back to ridgetop views; 5 miles out and back to Ellis Lake

Approximate hiking time: 1.5 hours to ridgetop; 3 hours to Ellis Lake

Difficulty: More challenging due to the 800-foot climb to the ridge

Trail surface: Rocky singletrack

Best seasons: Summer, fall

Other trail users: The occasional mountain biker; the occasional motorcycle rider

Canine compatibility: Leashed dogs permitted

Fees and permits: None

Schedule: Sunrise to sunset daily

Maps: USGS Homewood (CA); Lake Tahoe Basin Management Unit Map; Tom Harrison Recreation Map of Lake Tahoe

Trail contact: For the trail, contact USDA Forest Service Tahoe National Forest, 9646 Donner Pass Rd., Truckee, CA 96161; (530) 587-3558; www.fs.fed.us/r5/tahoe. For trailhead access via Barker Pass Road contact USDA Forest Service Lake Tahoe Basin Management Unit, Forest Supervisor's Office, 35 College Dr., South Lake Tahoe, CA 96150; (530) 543-2600; www.fs.fed.us/r5/ltbmu.

Special considerations: Given the trail's steepness and elevation gain, this arguably is not an easy hike (though it definitely qualifies as one of the best). Do not attempt if you have heart, respiratory, or knee problems. Barker Pass Road to the summit receives heavy winter snow and typically does not open until mid-June.

Finding the trailhead: From Tahoe City take CA 89 south for 4.1 miles to the turnoff marked for Kaspian and Blackwood Canyon. Turn right (west) onto Barker Pass Road. Stay left (south) where the road splits, crossing Blackwood Creek, and go about 7 miles to the signed trailhead on the left (west) side of the road just before the end of the pavement. Limited parking is available in pullouts along Barker Pass Road. No other amenities are available. GPS: N39 04.309' / W120 13.868'

The Hike

The splendor of the northern Sierra is powerfully displayed from a perch atop the rocky ridge crested by the Ellis Peak Trail. Cliffs drop sharply into the green valley of Blackwood Canyon, with Lake Tahoe a vast inky stain on the gray and green landscape. To the southwest lie the forbidding, gunmetal gray ramparts of the Desolation Wilderness, an impressive landscape of flowing granite, lingering snow-fields, and small, iridescent lakes.

Beyond this aerie, the Sierra shows yet another aspect of its makeup. Towering firs create a shady canopy overhead, and needles dense on the forest floor quiet the footfalls of hikers. The thunderhead-dark battlements of Ellis Peak rise above peaceful Ellis Lake, a pretty tarn in a classic alpine setting of evergreens and talus.

This hike begins with a relatively brutal climb up steep switchbacks. The views begin as you enter a ridgetop field with broad-leafed mule ear and wildflowers hunkering close to the ground. Tortured evergreens turn barren backsides to the prevailing west wind, forming a spindly windbreak as the route passes outcrops hovering over Blackwood Canyon.

Uninterrupted sunlight and tundra grasses blanket the high point. Wind-lashed trees hook over the trail; look for a side trail leading left (east) onto a lovely rock perch where 360-degree views can be enjoyed. This is the first turnaround point.

Beyond the overlook, the trail descends into forest. The drop begins gradually but grows steeper until the angle moderates amid thick, lichen-coated firs. Skirt a meadow on the right (west) side of the trail, then begin a gentle climb. The trail curls through a magnificent stand of old firs to a marked trail junction. Go left (east) on the gravel roadway, passing a shallow pond that lies in a depression on the left (north).

The final stretch skirts a talus field that spills from the cliffs of Ellis Peak to bottle-green Ellis Lake. A mixed fir forest circles three-quarters of the lake, but on the south shore a steep spill of talus pours into the water, and alpine scrub hugs the slope above the rockfall. Once you've enjoyed the lake's amenities, even taking a swim if the weather permits, return as you came.

Miles and Directions

0.0 Start by passing the trail sign and climbing steep switch-backs into the woods.

0.4 The climb eases as you reach a saddle with views of Lake Tahoe to the east, Loon Lake to the west, and the Desolation Wilderness to the southwest.

1.0 Follow the ridgeback up to where it mellows and offers view-points from overlook rocks. This is the first turnaround point. If you continue, follow the obvious route heading south, which begins to drop into the woods.

Ellis Peak Trail

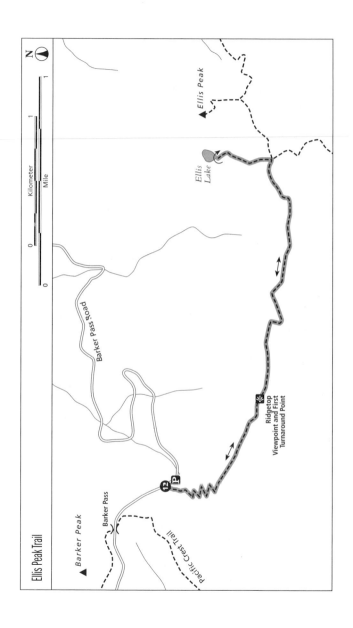

2.2 Reach the marked junction where the trail intersects a rough gravel road. Go left (north) on the roadway toward Ellis Lake. The singletrack that rises straight ahead (east) climbs to Ellis Peak. The road to the right (south) drops to the McKinney Rubicon Trail near Miller Meadows and Miller Lake.

2.5 Arrive at Ellis Lake. This is the second turnaround point; retrace your steps from here.

5.0 Return to the trailhead.

Options: Travel another 0.5 mile west on Barker Pass Road to the trailhead for the Pacific Crest Trail. A 3-mile out-and-back hike heading north on the PCT offers a sampling of the rigors and beauty of the national scenic trail. Rugged but well-maintained, user-friendly but not overcrowded, the singletrack offers wonderful views of Blackwood Canyon, Lake Tahoe, and the Desolation Wilderness. A plug of dark volcanic rock jutting from rose-colored earth marks the end of this recommended route, though you can follow the PCT all the way to Canada.

13 General Creek Loop at Sugar Pine Point State Park

Walk in the footsteps (or ski tracks) of Olympic biathletes along the General Creek Loop, which follows gentle General Creek into Sugar Pine Point State Park's wooded backcountry.

Distance: 4.7-mile lollipop
Approximate hiking time: 3 hours
Trail surface: Dirt forest roads; paved road
Best seasons: Spring, summer, fall
Other trail users: Mountain bikers, trail runners
Canine compatibility: Leashed dogs permitted
Fees and permits: Day-use fee
Schedule: The Sugar Pine State Park trail system is open for year-round recreation from sunrise to sunset daily. Entrance station hours vary; in summer it is open from about 8:00 a.m. until 8:00 p.m.
Maps: USGS Homewood, Meeks Bay (CA); map in the Sugar Pine Point State Park brochure available at the campground entrance station and online
Trail contact: Sugar Pine Point State Park, P.O. Box 266, Tahoma, CA 96142-0266; (530) 525-7982; www.parks.ca.gov

Finding the trailhead: From the Y junction of US 50 and CA 89 in South Lake Tahoe, follow CA 89 north for 17.5 miles to the signed entrance for Sugar Pine Point State Park. From the Y junction of CA 89 and CA 28 in Tahoe City, follow CA 89 south for 9.2 miles to the campground entrance on the left (west). Go left (south), behind the entrance station, to parking for the campground amphitheater. This is the day-use trailhead; restrooms, information, and water are available in the campground. GPS (day-use trailhead): N39 03.38' / W120 07.287'

The Hike

The biathlon has to be one of the most bizarre sporting events ever conceived. Cross-country skiing—an exhausting sport even when you are not racing—is paired with marksmanship; speed and accuracy determine the winner.

The General Creek Loop follows part of the route racers traversed in the 1960 Olympic Games, offering hikers a chance to gain a new appreciation for (or sense of astonishment at) the sport. Interpretive signs near the trailhead provide an introduction to the Nordic trail system established for the games. But the sign near the second bridge crossing General Creek, more than 2 miles into the woods, is a real eye-opener. The pictures say it all: Skiers sprawled belly-down in the snow with the rifles they've carried on their backs aimed at targets across the white meadow. Stand where they lay and try to comprehend . . .

The hike begins with a tour of the Sugar Pine Point campground. The most direct route to the trailhead proper is to follow the main campground road to the westernmost campground loop; the signed trail begins between campsites 76 and 125.

The dirt road that serves as the trail leads through a woodland cleared of underbrush. Pass a side trail that breaks left (south) into the campground, then follow the roadway to the start of the loop, going left (south) to the first General Creek crossing. A bridge spans the waterway; on the south side go right (west) on the gently climbing track.

Follow the creek westward for a meditative mile through the quiet forest and a burned area where the undergrowth is thick and lush. Bend north past the biathlon sign ("a contest of contrast") to the second General Creek crossing. On the

General Creek Loop at Sugar Pine Point State Park

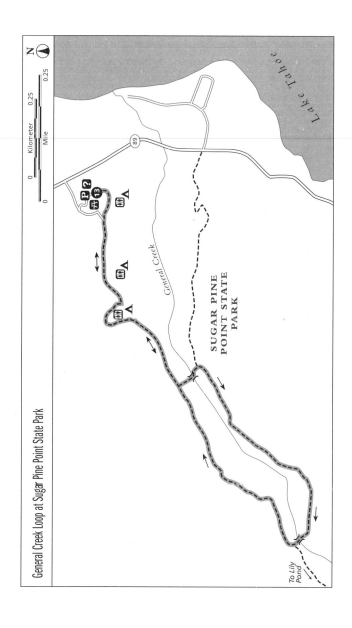

north side of the bridge, the singletrack Lily Pond Trail heads left (west). Stay right on the broad General Creek Loop, which follows the north side of the creek through an old burn where wildflowers, thimbleberries, and ferns flourish in spring and early summer.

Pass an unmarked junction with another dirt road on the descent, staying right (east). The trail/road drops to close the loop; from that point retrace your steps to the campground trailhead, then through the camp to the day-use parking lot and trail's end.

Miles and Directions

0.0 Start in the amphitheater parking lot, passing behind the closed gate on the paved roadway. Ski trail and nature trail signs mark a convergence of paved paths. Stay right on the paved trail to the main camp road, then go left (west) on the camp road.

0.9 Arrive at the signed General Creek trailhead, between campsites 76 and 125. Head down the wide graded dirt road into the woods.

1.0 Pass a side trail that leads left (south) into the campground. Stay straight on the main trail.

1.4 At the trail junction (the start of the loop) go left (south). Cross the bridge over the creek. At the trail intersection on the south bank, turn right (west).

2.4 Pass the biathlon sign and cross the creek via the bridge. The Lily Pond Trail heads left (west) on the north side of the bridge; stay right (east) on the General Creek trail.

3.1 At the unsigned junction with dirt road, stay right (east).

3.4 Close the loop. Retrace your steps to the campground trailhead.

4.7 Arrive back at the amphitheater parking area.

14 The Lighthouse and Rubicon Point

Though the historic lighthouse on Rubicon Point may be the "high point" of this loop, panoramic views and a stretch of trail that skims a rocky cliff above the lake vie for the top spot.

Distance: 2.5-mile loop
Approximate hiking time: 2 hours
Difficulty: Moderate due to elevation changes
Trail surface: Singletrack; rock staircases
Best seasons: Late spring, summer, fall
Other trail users: None
Canine compatibility: Leashed dogs permitted in the park; no dogs permitted on the trails

Fees and permits: Day-use fee
Schedule: Trail available sunrise to sunset daily; visitor center hours are from 10:00 a.m. to 4:00 p.m. daily
Maps: USGS Emerald Bay (CA); map provided in the D. L. Bliss State Park brochure
Trail contact: D. L. Bliss State Park, P.O. Box 266, Tahoma, CA 96142; (530) 525-7277; www .parks.ca.gov

Finding the trailhead: From the intersection of US 50 and CA 89 in South Lake Tahoe, head north on CA 89 for 12.5 miles to the signed turnoff for D. L. Bliss State Park on the right (east). From Tahoe City, take CA 89 south for 15.8 miles to the park entrance. Follow the park road 1 mile east to the trailhead, which is on the left (west) side of the road. A limited number of visitors are admitted into the park; if you arrive after 10:00 a.m., check at the visitor center or entrance station for availability. Restrooms, information, and picnic facilities are available in the park. GPS: N39 59.353' / W120 05.915'

The Hike

The lighthouse that once warned sailors of submerged dangers off Rubicon Point is startlingly small and unassuming. It resembles, of all the unfortunate possibilities, an old-time wooden outhouse. But in the early days of the twentieth century, it housed a brilliant acetylene light that was integral to navigation on the lake. Though rebuilt in 2001, the light no longer shines on boaters, but the structure definitely enlivens this loop though D. L. Bliss State Park.

The lighthouse isn't the only example of rugged construction along this route. Climbing away from Calawee Cove, the trail skims a steep rocky face high above the lake. Views from this aerie are superlative and the exposure is thrilling. A word of caution: Though protected by a railing, this stretch is not for those afraid of heights, and children should be watched carefully.

The Lighthouse Trail begins by climbing through a fire-scarred woodland. It flattens atop a ridge amid evergreens and boulders, then drops through more hauntingly beautiful burned forest. Drop to a trail junction with great views. The granite staircase leading to the lighthouse is to the left and descends steeply to the small wooden structure, which is perched on a rocky shelf overlooking the lake.

Climb back to the trail crossing and go right (north) on the Lighthouse Trail, which follows long, shaded switchbacks down to the paved parking area at Calawee Cove. The cove's little beach is below the lot; the signed junction with the Rubicon Trail is to the right (south). Pick up that footpath and head up around the point.

The trail is spectacularly exposed for a stretch, with a rail guarding against the abrupt drop, boardwalks spanning

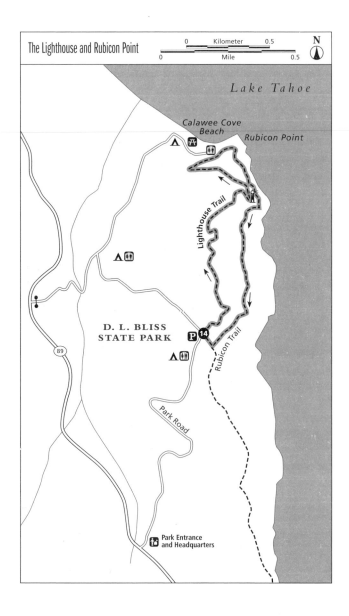

The Lighthouse and Rubicon Point

| 0 | Kilometer | 0.5 |
| 0 | Mile | 0.5 |

N

Lake Tahoe

Calawee Cove
Beach

Rubicon Point

Lighthouse Trail

D. L. BLISS
STATE PARK

P 14

Rubicon Trail

Park Road

Park Entrance
and Headquarters

89

clefts, and head-thumping overhangs looming over the trail. It's so invigorating you might forget you are climbing . . . until you reach the granite staircase heading up and past a trail leading to the lighthouse. Stay left (south) on the Rubicon Trail, enjoying heavenly views as the trail flattens.

As you near the end of the trail, it curves away from the lake into dense forest. At the signed trail junction in a clearing, take the trail to the right (northwest); the left-hand trail leads south to Emerald Bay and Vikingsholm. The dark, needle-carpeted path leads to the park road and the neighboring Lighthouse trailhead.

Miles and Directions

0.0   Start at the signed Lighthouse trailhead, crossing a small bridge and climbing into a burned woodland.

0.7   Drop to a trail intersection. Go left (north) for about 10 feet to an interpretive sign and the top of the stone staircase leading down to the lighthouse.

0.8   Arrive at the lighthouse. Check it out, then climb back to the Lighthouse Trail and turn right (north).

1.4   Descend to the parking lot and restrooms at Calawee Cove. Pick up the signed Rubicon Trail and head right (south).

1.6   Reach the exposed part of the trail, with the wire rail, boardwalk, rock faces, and great views.

1.8   Climb the granite staircase up to and past the trail to the lighthouse, staying left (south) on the Rubicon.

2.1   Pass a trailside overlook.

2.4   Reach the clearing and trail junction. Go right (west) to the park road and trailhead.

2.5   Arrive back at the trailhead.

15 Vikingsholm and Emerald Point

A summertime trip to Lake Tahoe wouldn't be complete without a visit to Emerald Bay. Ocean-green and opalescent, it's quite obvious how this gleaming arm of Tahoe earned its name. Spectacular Vikingsholm, at the head of the bay, is the obvious destination for most visitors. Not so obvious is the jewel of a trail that leads along the shore to the bay's narrow mouth.

Distance: 5.2 miles out and back
Approximate hiking time: 3 hours
Difficulty: More challenging due to elevation change and trail length
Trail surface: Graded dirt road; pavement; singletrack
Best seasons: Spring, summer, fall
Other trail users: None
Canine compatibility: Leashed dogs permitted in the park; no dogs allowed on trails or beaches, or at Vikingsholm
Fees and permits: Parking fee
Schedule: The trail is open from sunrise to sunset. Vikingsholm and the Emerald Bay State Park visitor center are open daily from Memorial Day to September 30 from 10:00 a.m. to 4:00 p.m. Tours of Vikingsholm are available for a fee; call (530) 541-3030.

Maps: USGS Emerald Bay (CA); Emerald Bay park map and brochure available online and at the visitor center
Trail contact: Emerald Bay State Park, P.O. Box 266, Tahoma, CA 96142; (530) 541-3030 (summer only); www.parks.ca.gov
Special considerations: The highway and parking lots at Vikingsholm and neighboring Eagle Falls are congested during high season. Lots fill quickly, with additional parking available along the roadway. Please be courteous and safe in selecting a parking space. You will gain and lose more than 400 feet in elevation within the first mile. Heed the trailhead sign that warns you not to attempt the route if you have heart, respiratory, or knee problems.

Finding the trailhead: From the intersection of US 50 and CA 89 in South Lake Tahoe, head north on CA 89 for 10.7 miles to the large Emerald Bay State Park parking area on the right (southeast). From Tahoe City, take CA 89 south for 17.6 miles (parking is on the left). The signed trail begins to the left of the huge rock slab that overlooks Emerald Bay. There's a gift and information station in the parking lot; restrooms, a visitor center, and picnic facilities are at Vikingsholm. GPS: N38 57.261' / W120 06.619'

The Hike

Of all the shoreline estates along Lake Tahoe, Vikingsholm is arguably the most spectacular, with striking Scandinavian architecture and views onto sparkling Emerald Bay and rocky Fannette Island. Lora Josephine Knight built the home in 1929; she also built the little castle-like tea house on the summit of Fannette Island (the only island in Lake Tahoe). The house, designed by architect Lennart Palme, Mrs. Knight's nephew, features massive carved timbers, massive granite boulders mortared into exterior walls, and a roof sewn with wildflowers.

Hiking down to visit the storied estate is a quintessential and massively popular excursion. But stretch a bit beyond the estate along the Rubicon Trail and you can enjoy Emerald Bay in relative solitude. Walk quietly and watchfully as you near Emerald Point; you may see an eagle or osprey return to a lakeside nest, a tangle of twigs and branches perched at the top of a standing dead tree.

Begin by heading down the wide path (a human highway in the busy summer season). Two switchbacks broken with long traverses drop to a junction where a park map points you downhill and right through open woodland to Vikingsholm. Take some time to explore the grounds, visit

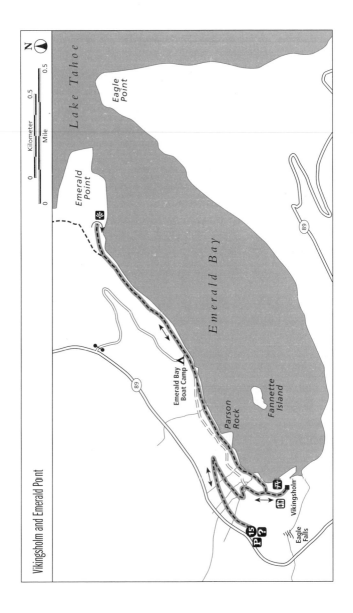

Vikingsholm and Emerald Point

N

Lake Tahoe

Eagle Point

Emerald Point

Emerald Bay

89

Emerald Bay Boat Camp

Parson Rock

Fannette Island

Vikingsholr

P 15
?

Eagle Falls

89

0   0.5
Kilometer

0   0.5
Mile

the visitor center, take a tour of the house, and picnic on the beach. When you're ready to move on, pick up the signed Rubicon Trail on the northeast side of the main house (the right side as you face the building from the beach).

A series of bridges and boardwalks assist passage along the forested shoreline trail, which is intersected by drainages and lush with berries, ferns, and other verdant undergrowth. It's easy going to Parson Rock, which overlooks the bay and Fannette Island just before the trail enters the Emerald Bay Boat Camp.

The Rubicon merges with the camp road for a stretch, then breaks back to the shoreline as a dirt singletrack at a trail sign. The easy rambling continues, with short timber stair steps leading down to half-moon beaches along the waterline. The mouth of the bay, pinched by Emerald Point on the north and Eagle Point on the south, remains in sight until the Rubicon begins to bend north toward Rubicon Bay and Calawee Cove. A clearing just before the trail heads north is the turnaround point (though any of the little beaches would work just as well). Return as you came, enjoying sporadic views up into the stony Desolation Wilderness as you go.

Miles and Directions

Note: Mileages include a 0.3-mile tour of the paved paths around Vikingsholm.

- **0.0** Start by descending the broad, well-graded trail.
- **1.0** Arrive at Vikingsholm and tour the grounds.
- **1.3** A signed trailhead for the Rubicon Trail is to the right (northeast) of Vikingsholm as you face it. Turn right (east) onto the flat path.

1.9 Enter the boat camp and follow the paved road through the campsites.

2.1 At the east end of the camp, where the pavement begins to climb, the signed Rubicon Trail breaks to the right (east), turning to dirt and following the shoreline.

2.4 Pass a series of short staircases that lead down to tiny beaches.

2.6 Reach a clearing where trails appear to split, with the obvious Rubicon Trail breaking left (north). This is the turnaround point. The social tracks dead-end in the brush. Retrace your steps back toward the trailhead.

5.2 Arrive back at the trailhead.

Option: The Rubicon Trail continues through neighboring D. L. Bliss State Park to Rubicon Point, a 4.5-mile one-way journey from Vikingsholm.

16 Eagle Lake

Dark and clear, Eagle Lake sits in a basin bordered by talus slopes and great black-streaked cliffs. A small island sits slightly off-center in its midst, isolated by frigid mountain water. The classic Sierran setting makes it clear why this is one of the most popular hikes around Lake Tahoe.

Distance: 2 miles out and back
Approximate hiking time: 1 hour
Difficulty: More challenging due to some steep climbing
Trail surface: Dirt singletrack; granite stair steps
Best seasons: Summer and fall
Other trail users: None
Canine compatibility: Leashed dogs permitted. Because the trail is so popular, owners need to keep their pets under control.
Fees and permits: Per-vehicle parking fee, if you can find space in the lot. Parking along CA 89 is free. A free wilderness permit, available at the trailhead, is required.
Schedule: Sunrise to sunset daily
Maps: USGS Emerald Bay (CA); Lake Tahoe Basin Management Unit Map; Tom Harrison's Recreation Map of Lake Tahoe
Trail contact: USDA Forest Service Lake Tahoe Basin Management Unit, Forest Supervisor's Office, 35 College Dr., South Lake Tahoe, CA 96150; (530) 543-2600; www.fs.fed.us/r5/ltbmu
Special considerations: The highway and parking lots at Eagle Falls and neighboring Vikingsholm are congested during the high season. Parking lots fill quickly, with additional parking available along the highway. Please be courteous and safe in selecting a parking space.

You will gain and lose about 400 feet in elevation, and must climb and descend a stretch of granite steps, so be prepared for a moderate workout.

Finding the trailhead: From the intersection of US 50 and CA 89 in South Lake Tahoe, head north on CA 89 for 10.3 miles to the signed Eagle Falls parking area on the left (south). From Tahoe City follow CA 89 south for 18 miles, past the parking area for Vikingsholm, to the Eagle Falls parking lot on the right. The well-signed trailhead is near the picnic area and restrooms. GPS: N38 57.118' / W120 06.811'

The Hike

The bare, cathedral-like walls of a stark Desolation Wilderness cirque form the backdrop for Eagle Lake. The trail leading up to the lake is varied and moderately challenging but quite short, making it well within reach of any hiker seeking an alpine experience without excess effort.

Begin on stairs at the trailhead sign, staying on the signed Eagle Lake Trail where it connects with the shorter Eagle Loop. The trail climbs gently at first, allowing you to enjoy views of Eagle Falls and the soaring pinnacles and great gray domes of the Desolation Wilderness.

Nearing the cascade, a twisting stone stairway leads up, then down, to a vista point and the sturdy bridge spanning the cataract. Cross the bridge and climb granite stairs and rocky singletrack past the wilderness boundary sign and to a large, smooth granite slab dotted with pine and cedar. The trail is worn into the slab; rocks line the track as well.

The trail skirts a rock outcrop overlooking the lush creekbed below, then traverses above the drainage on a well-worn wooded path, with the jagged crowns of the canyon walls rising above the forest. Gentle climbing takes you to a trail junction at 0.9 mile; from here you can head deeper into the Desolation Wilderness. To reach Eagle Lake, however, bear right (west) toward the giant cirque, following the arrow on the sign.

Eagle Lake

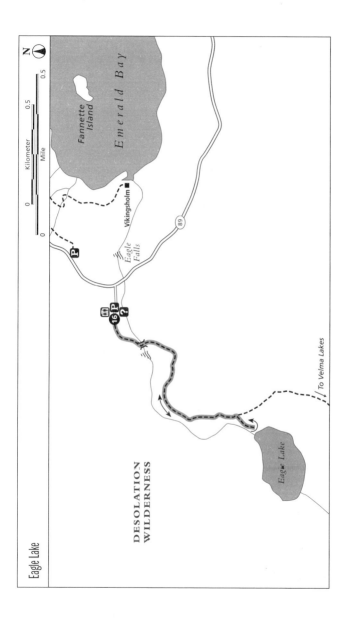

N

0   Kilometer   0.5

0   Mile   0.5

Fannette Island

Emerald Bay

Vikingsholm ■

Eagle Falls

89

16 P ?

P

DESOLATION
WILDERNESS

Eagle Lake

To Velma Lakes

Scramble down to the shores of Eagle Lake at 1.0 mile. A sprinkling of cedar, ponderosa, and Jeffrey pine provide shade from the vivid alpine sunshine. If you don't mind icy water, Eagle Lake invites a dip. There is no beach, however, so you'll have to dry off and/or enjoy the stunning views from a perch on a tree stump or a sunbaked granite slab.

Return the way you came, enjoying lake views on the descent.

Miles and Directions

0.0 Start by climbing steps to the junction of the Eagle Lake Trail and the Eagle Loop. Stay left (southwest) on the Eagle Lake Trail.

0.2 Climb granite steps past the second Eagle Loop trail junction and stay left (south), crossing the bridge.

0.4 Pass the Desolation Wilderness boundary.

0.9 At the junction with the trail to Velma Lakes, stay right (south) on the signed trail to Eagle Lake.

1.0 Arrive at Eagle Lake. Enjoy the scenery, then retrace your steps back to the trailhead

2.0 Arrive back at the trailhead.

Options: From the trail intersection just before Eagle Lake, you can head into the far reaches of the Desolation Wilderness. The nearest destination is the Velma Lakes (5 miles from the Eagle Falls trailhead), but the wilderness offers an abundance of hiking and backpacking possibilities.

17 Cascade Falls

A brief, quiet ramble through nicely spaced evergreens is a peaceful preamble to the rocky path and raucous creek at trail's end. Views of Cascade Lake and Lake Tahoe add to the hike's appeal.

Distance: 2 miles out and back
Approximate hiking time: 1.5 hours
Difficulty: More challenging due to climbs and descents over rocky terrain
Trail surface: Dirt singletrack; granite
Best seasons: Late spring, summer, fall
Other trail users: None
Canine compatibility: Leashed dogs permitted
Fees and permits: None
Schedule: Sunrise to sunset daily

Maps: USGS Emerald Bay (CA); Lake Tahoe Basin Management Unit Map; Tom Harrison Recreation Map of Lake Tahoe
Trail contact: USDA Forest Service Lake Tahoe Basin Management Unit, Forest Supervisor's Office, 35 College Dr., South Lake Tahoe, CA 96150; (530) 543-2600; www.fs .fed.us/r5/ltbmu
Other: Though the total elevation change is only about 80 feet, the trail traverses some steep, rocky terrain. Do not attempt if you have heart, respiratory, or knee problems.

Finding the trailhead: From the intersection of US 50 and CA 89 in South Lake Tahoe, head north on CA 89 for 9.4 miles to a left (south) turn into the Bayview Campground. From Tahoe City follow CA 89 south for 18.9 miles, past the parking areas for Vikingsholm and Eagle Falls, to a right turn into the campground. Follow the campground road 0.3 mile to limited parking at the signed trailhead. Direct access to the trailhead may be difficult in high season; be prepared to park outside the campground or in safe pullouts along

the highway. Restrooms and information are available in the campground. GPS: N38 56.607' / W120 06.000'

The Hike

Though not in view until the end of the trail, boisterous
Cascade Creek feeds both Cascade Falls and Cascade Lake.
The dark, still lake, cupped in a wooded bowl and surrounded by private property, is off-limits to hikers. The
falls are off-limits too, rendered inaccessible by steep granite
faces. But above the falls the creek is friendlier to visitors,
coursing over smooth granite slabs. Settle in on the sunny
rocks and enjoy the cooling mists while taking in vistas of
Cascade Lake and Lake Tahoe.

To begin, walk behind the information kiosk and turn
left (south) onto Cascade Trail. The trail bends around two
short trail posts in the mixed evergreen forest, then climbs
a short, stone stairway to overlook the falls, Cascade Lake,
and Lake Tahoe.

At about the 0.5-mile mark, the trail begins a rocky
downward traverse of the slope on the north side of Cascade
Lake. Pick your way down to and then along the base of a
granite cliff, taking care as the footing is uneven. You can
catch glimpses of the falls tumbling toward the lake, but
make sure you stop before you look.

Cross a relatively narrow ledge, then climb granite steps
and broken rock to the broad sunsplashed slabs that cradle the
creek. A lovely granite bowl opens upstream, stretching back
into Desolation Wilderness. A maze of trails has been worked
onto the landscape over the years, some marked by "ducks"
(stacks of rocks sometimes called cairns) and others delineated
by lines of rocks. Look left and downhill for a wooden trail
marker that points the way to the falls overlook. Stay low (left

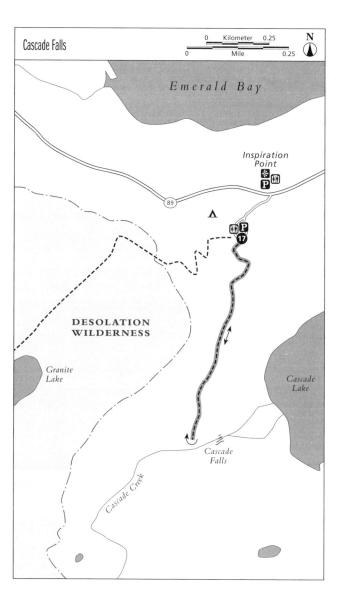

Cascade Falls

0   Kilometer   0.25

0   Mile   0.25

N

Emerald Bay

*Inspiration
Point*

89

*Granite
Lake*

**DESOLATION
WILDERNESS**

*Cascade
Lake*

*Cascade
Falls*

Cascade Creek

and north) to get closer to the falls, but don't get too close as you don't want to take a tumble near the cliff face. Stay high (right and south) to reach stretches of the creek that permit water play and toe-dipping.

The whole terrace opens on wonderful views. Take in the sights then return as you came.

Miles and Directions

0.0 Start behind the informational signboard, turning left (south) at the sign pointing toward Cascade Falls.

0.5 Head up the stone steps to lake views and vistas of the falls.

0.7 Traverse across slabs and steps at the base of a granite wall.

0.8 The trail levels as you approach the creek, and the granite cirque opens uphill to the south.

1.0 Reach the creek above the falls. Enjoy the sun and views, then return as you came.

2.0 Arrive back at the trailhead.

Option: A right (southwest) turn at the trailhead puts you on the trail to Granite Lake in the Desolation Wilderness. A wilderness permit for day use is required and available at the trailhead.

18 Rainbow Trail

The Taylor Creek Stream Profile Chamber is the main attraction along this popular route, but there's much more to recommend the Rainbow Trail, including vistas across the marsh surrounding Taylor Creek, bowers of quaking aspen, and comprehensive interpretive signage.

Distance: 0.6-mile loop
Approximate hiking time: 45 minutes
Difficulty: Easy
Trail surface: Paved path
Best seasons: Spring, summer, fall
Other trail users: None
Canine compatibility: Dogs not permitted in the stream chamber or on Kiva Beach, but otherwise allowed on leashes
Fees and permits: None
Schedule: The stream profile chamber is open Memorial Day to October 31 from 8:00 a.m. until a half-hour before the Taylor Creek Visitor Center closes. The visitor center is open from 8:00 a.m. to 4:30 p.m. from mid-May to mid-June and during October. It is open from 8:00 a.m. to 5:30 p.m. from mid-June through September.
Maps: USGS Emerald Bay (CA); but a map is not needed
Trail contact: USDA Forest Service Lake Tahoe Basin Management Unit, Forest Supervisor's Office, 35 College Dr., South Lake Tahoe, CA 96150; (530) 543-2600; www.fs .fed.us/r5/ltbmu
Special considerations: The trail is wheelchair accessible.

Finding the trailhead: From the intersection of US 50 and CA 89 in South Lake Tahoe, go north on CA 89 for 3.2 miles to the signed turnoff for the Taylor Creek Visitor Center. Turn right (north) onto the visitor center road, and follow it to the parking area. The trailhead, with an arcing sign, is opposite the visitor center entrance. Ample parking, restrooms, information, and gifts are available. GPS: N38 56.133' / W120 03.243'

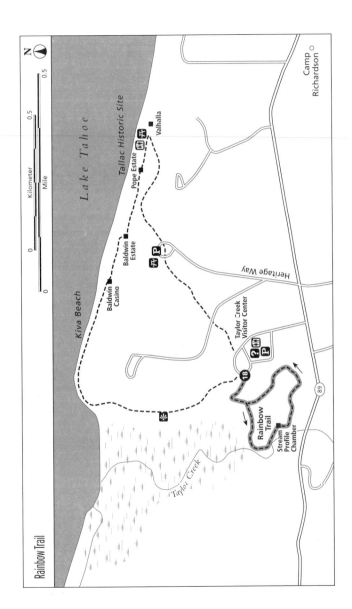

Rainbow Trail

N

Lake Tahoe

Kiva Beach

Tallac Historic Site

Baldwin Casino

Baldwin Estate

Pope Estate

Valhalla

Camp Richardson

Taylor Creek Visitor Center

Heritage Way

Rainbow Trail

Stream Profile Chamber

Taylor Creek

18

1

89

Kilometer

Mile

0.5

0.5

0

The Hike

In the clear water behind the glass of the Taylor Creek Stream Profile Chamber, kokanee salmon, their scales lipstick red as they prepare to spawn in autumn, seem to pace in lovesick agitation. They mingle with their cousins: rainbow, brown, and Lahontan cutthroat trout, the last species native to the deep waters of Lake Tahoe. Larger fish circle lazily in the stream while the smaller dart about swiftly, looking for food or perhaps hoping to avoid becoming a meal themselves.

The people stand on the other side of the glass, gazing in wonder at this snapshot of life in a mountain stream. Firsthand observation, coupled with the assistance of naturalist and additional information from the accompanying interpretive display, round out a unique hiking experience.

Though the stream profile chamber is the Rainbow Trail's main draw, this pleasant walk—easy enough for a toddler to manage—sports many other attractions. The marsh surrounding Taylor Creek is no scenic slouch, resplendent with wildflowers in spring and ringing with birdcall throughout the hiking season. Quaking aspen, turning as vivid a gold as the kokanee's red in fall, provide yet another visual lollipop. The route is lined with interpretive signs and benches, perfect tools to entertain and support children of all ages.

The path begins just outside the visitor center, dropping to a marsh overlook and then to a trail junction where the loop begins. Go right (following the arrow), traveling in a counterclockwise direction. Meander through the meadow and skirt the marsh on boardwalks, pausing to take in views toward Lake Tahoe and read the interpretive signs. A bridge spans Taylor Creek, then the trail forks, with one branch leading down and through the stream profile chamber and the other going around.

On the far side of the chamber, amid the aspen, pass a "pillow sensor" and rain gauge, and an interpretive display that explains their functions. Beyond lies an alder spring, and then the tall grasses and wildflowers of the meadow accompany you back to the trail fork. Go right to the visitor center and parking area.

Miles and Directions

0.0 Start on the paved path under the Rainbow Trail arch.

0.1 Visit the marsh overlook, then return to the trail and drop to the start of the loop. Go right (counterclockwise) as indicated by the arrow on the small sign.

0.3 Drop through the stream profile chamber.

0.4 At the Y outside the chamber, go left, past the monitoring station. Close the loop by circling back toward the visitor center.

0.6 Arrive back at the trailhead.

19 Lake of the Sky Trail and Tallac Historic Site

This flat, scenic loop links the natural history of Lake Tahoe to its human history, from the wild creatures that inhabit the Taylor Creek Marsh to turn-of-the-twentieth-century resort owners and their spectacular vacation homes.

Distance: 2.0-mile loop
Approximate hiking time: 1 hour
Trail surface: Singletrack; sand; pavement
Best seasons: Late spring, summer, fall
Other trail users: Cyclists, trail runners
Canine compatibility: No dogs permitted on the portion of Kiva Beach west of Kiva Point. Leashed dogs are allowed on the section of beach that is part of the Kiva Picnic Area. Though leashed dogs are allowed on the trails, Tallac Historic Site is not dog-friendly.
Fees and permits: None
Schedule: The Taylor Creek Visitor Center is open from 8:00

a.m. to 4:30 p.m. from mid-May to mid-June and during October. It is open from 8:00 a.m. to 5:30 p.m. from mid-June through September. The trails can be used from sunrise to sunset daily.
Maps: USGS Emerald Bay (CA); Lake Tahoe Basin Management Unit Map; Tom Harrison Recreation Map of Lake Tahoe
Trail contact: USDA Forest Service Lake Tahoe Basin Management Unit, Forest Supervisor's Office, 35 College Dr., South Lake Tahoe, CA 96150; (530) 543-2600; www.fs .fed.us/r5/ltbmu
Other: The link from the end of Lake of the Sky Trail to the Tallac Historic Site is not a formal forest service trail.

Finding the trailhead: From the intersection of US 50 and CA 89 in South Lake Tahoe, go north on CA 89 for 3.2 miles to the signed turnoff for the Taylor Creek Visitor Center. Turn right (north) onto the

Lake of the Sky Trail and Tallac Historic Site

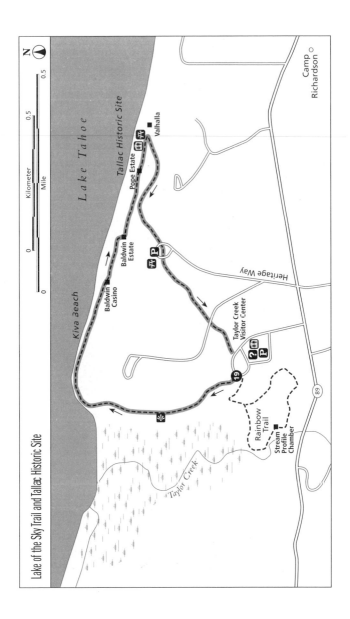

Lake Tahoe

Kiva Beach

Tallac Historic Site

Baldwin Casino

Baldwin Estate

Pope Estate

Valhalla

Taylor Creek Visitor Center

Heritage Way

Taylor Creek

Rainbow Trail

Stream Profile Chamber

Camp Richardson

89

N

Kilometer

Mile

0   0.5

0   0.5

visitor center road, and follow it to the parking area for the visitor center. The signed trailhead is on the north side of the visitor center. Ample parking, restrooms, information, and gifts are available. GPS: N38 56.165' / W120 03.228'

The Hike

Lake Tahoe has proven itself the perfect habitat for a variety of residents, from the Washoe Indians who summered on its shores to turn-of-the-twentieth-century vacationers who built grand estates and party palaces . . . not to mention the myriad wild creatures—deer, eagles, and trout, to name a few—that have called the lake home for thousands of years. This trail loop offers glimpses into what each found and left on Tahoe's shores.

The tour begins on the Lake of the Sky Trail, which heads north from the Taylor Creek Visitor Center along the Taylor Creek Marsh to Kiva Beach. The trail is lined with interpretive signs and boasts a viewing deck overlooking Taylor Marsh.

At Kiva Beach the formal trail ends, and an informal trail leads east along the beach toward more developed trails in the Tallac Historic Site. Wander down along the water, watching the boaters, then hitch right (south) up one of the short staircases onto the doubletrack that leads eastward into the historic site.

Pass the foundations of the Tallac Resort Casino in the woodland lining the shore; an interpretive sign describes the ballroom, gambling rooms, bowling alley, and stage that "Lucky" Baldwin built and operated on the site. Baldwin's purchase of the lakefront property in 1880 also resulted in the preservation of the grand old Jeffrey pines that shade picnic areas along the trail.

The trail bends right (south) at a gate to the signed TAL-LAC MUSEUM and WASHOE INDIAN EXHIBIT. Inside the Tallac Historic Site, you can wander at will through the grounds of the Baldwin, Pope, and Heller estates. Interpretive signs describe the buildings—cabins, homes, a museum, a boathouse theater—and exhibits preserved at the site, all of which have tree-screened lake views. Spend an hour here or the rest of the day, but be sure to visit the wonderful arboretum and garden before you head out to the parking lot to complete the loop.

A sign at the north end of the historic site's parking area directs you onto the singletrack trail that leads through scrub and woodland back to the visitor center and trailhead.

Miles and Directions

0.0 Begin on the signed, paved Lake of the Sky Trail on the north side of the visitor center. Pass the amphitheater; the trail turns to dirt.

0.2 Visit the viewing platform.

0.4 Reach the end of the Lake of the Sky Trail (with a map) at Kiva Beach. Turn right (east) along the beach.

0.6 Go right (south) up one of the short staircases onto the trail that parallels the beach. Go left (east) along the doubletrack past the Baldwin casino.

0.9 The trail bends right (south) to the first buildings of the Tallac Historic Site. Go left, into the Washoe Indian exhibit, then wander through the historic site.

1.7 Complete your tour in the main parking lot. The signed singletrack back to the Taylor Creek Visitor Center is on the north side of the lot.

1.8 Cross the park road.

2.0 Arrive back at the trailhead.

20 Cathedral Lake

Statuesque Mount Tallac, which dominates nearly every South Lake Tahoe vista, is an especially powerful presence on this hike. Cathedral Lake lies at the terminus of one of the peak's many talus fields, a peaceful tarn cupped in jumbled rock and thick-trunked evergreens.

Distance: 5.6 miles out and back
Approximate hiking time: 4 hours
Difficulty: More challenging due to an 1,100-foot elevation gain
Trail surface: Dirt singletrack
Best seasons: Late spring, summer, early fall
Other trail users: None
Canine compatibility: Leashed dogs permitted
Fees and permits: A free wilderness permit is required and available at the trailhead.

Schedule: Sunrise to sunset
Maps: USGS Emerald Bay (CA); Lake Tahoe Basin Management Unit Map; Tom Harrison Recreation Map of Lake Tahoe
Trail contact: USDA Forest Service Lake Tahoe Basin Management Unit, Forest Supervisor's Office, 35 College Dr., South Lake Tahoe, CA 96150; (530) 543-2600; www.fs.fed.us/r5/ltbmu
Special considerations: Do not attempt this climb if you have heart, respiratory, or knee problems.

Finding the trailhead: From the intersection of US 50 and CA 89 in South Lake Tahoe, head north on CA 89 for 4.1 miles to the turnoff for Camp Shelly and the Mount Tallac trailhead. Turn left (west) onto the trailhead road, and drive 0.4 mile to the first fork in the road, signed for the Mount Tallac trailhead and Camp Concord. Go left (southwest) for 0.2 mile to another intersection. Stay straight (right) on FR 1306, again signed for the Mount Tallac trailhead. The parking area is 0.5 mile ahead. No facilities other than an information signboard are provided. GPS: N38 55.283' / W120 04.086'

The Hike

Separated from its gray-green flanks by a narrow glacial valley for most of the hike, every foot of the Mount Tallac Trail to Cathedral Lake is shadowed by the daunting rampart of Mount Tallac. Though the elevation gain is significant, the climbing is never painfully steep and is mitigated by great views, shade, and the chance to rest and refuel at Floating Island Lake. The ultimate destination is Cathedral Lake, set in a talus-rimmed bowl near treeline on the mountain's southeast flank.

The trail begins by climbing through sunny scrubland scented with sage. Ascend a couple of switchbacks and wonderful views open of Fallen Leaf Lake below (east), and Lake Tahoe, behind and to the north.

The views improve atop the narrow ridgeback of the lateral moraine separating Fallen Leaf Lake from Mount Tallac, with the trail cruising along the spine of the moraine through Jeffrey pine and mountain hemlock. Drop off the ridge into a drainage, where the views are abandoned for shade.

The trail rollercoasters through forest and gully as it veers north into the shadow of the mountain. Climb up to and then alongside the creek that issues from Floating Island Lake. Enter the Desolation Wilderness then hitch up a final stretch to the flat, quiet shoreline of the little lake.

The trail skirts the forested south shore of Floating Island Lake. At the edge of a small talus field just above the lake, the trail veers right (west), resuming the climb via a short staircase composed of blocks of granite from the talus. Cross a small meadow and a creek (stay left on the main trail); beyond, the trail traverses a hillside that is strewn with wildflowers and butterflies in early summer.

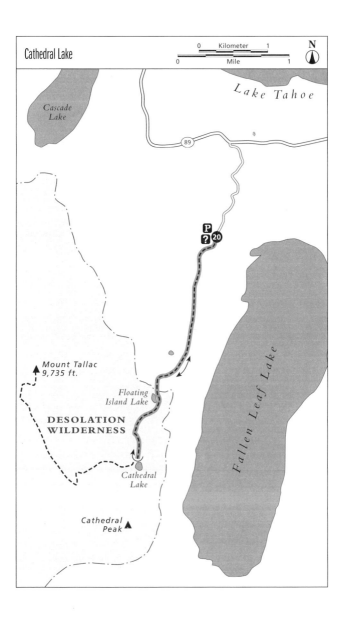

Cathedral Lake

Drop to a second creek crossing, then meander up to the junction with a trail that descends to Fallen Leaf Lake. Stay right (southwest), climbing a last pitch up to Cathedral Lake. Rest on the shores of the small tarn, then return to the trailhead by the same route.

Miles and Directions

0.0 Start up the trail behind the informational signboard.

0.7 Reach the top of the lateral moraine with views down to Fallen Leaf Lake and Lake Tahoe, and up to Mount Tallac.

1.2 Drop off the moraine.

1.8 Climb up along a creek to the boundary of the Desolation Wilderness.

1.9 Arrive at Floating Island Lake.

2.5 Cross a streamlet and stay right (west) around the talus field.

2.7 Arrive at the signed junction with the trail to Fallen Leaf Lake. Stay right (south) and up on the Mount Tallac Trail.

2.8 Arrive at Cathedral Lake. Rest, then retrace your steps.

5.6 Arrive back at the trailhead.

Options: If you've the will and strength, you can make the steep climb to the summit of Mount Tallac (9,735 feet; about 2.4 miles beyond Cathedral Lake).

Nearby Grass Lake is another appealing destination below Mount Tallac. With two lakes, two waterfalls, and three creek crossings, the stretch of the Glen Alpine Trail from Lily Lake to Grass Lake is invigorating. To reach the trailhead, follow Fallen Leaf Lake Road west for 5 miles to a fork. Go left (west) on FR 1216, signed for Lily Lake. The trailhead parking area is 0.6 mile ahead, marked by a green metal gate. A free wilderness permit is required for day use.

21 Lam Watah Nature Trail

Wind through alternating meadow and open Jeffrey pine forest from Stateline's busy casino district to Lake Tahoe's sparkling Nevada Beach.

Distance: 2.3 miles out and back
Approximate hiking time: 1.5 hours
Difficulty: Easy
Trail surface: Decomposed granite trail; asphalt; sand
Best seasons: Spring, summer, fall
Other trail users: Mountain bikers, trail runners
Canine compatibility: Leashed dogs permitted on trail; no dogs allowed on Nevada Beach
Fees and permits: None
Schedule: Sunrise to sunset daily
Maps: USGS South Lake Tahoe (CV, NV)
Trail contact: USDA Forest Service Lake Tahoe Basin Management Unit, Forest Supervisor's Office, 35 College Dr., South Lake Tahoe, CA 96150; (530) 543-2600; www.fs.fed.us/r5/ltbmu

Finding the trailhead: The trailhead is just northeast of Stateline's casino district at the corner of US 50 and Kahle Drive. Turn left (north) onto Kahle Drive then immediately right into the small parking lot with an informational signboard. There are no amenities at the trailhead, but restrooms are in the campground at Nevada Beach. GPS: N38 58.251' / W119 56.151'

The Hike

Linking the busy strip at Stateline with scenic Nevada Beach, the Lam Watah Trail is a peaceful interlude. The setting alternates between swatches of meadow and open pine woodland, a wide and gentle walk–and–talk route perfect for a sunset stroll or a break from the gaming tables.

Though the route never wanders far from civilization—houses are visible along Kahle Road at the outset and the towers of the casinos and the Heavenly Valley gondola rise against the mountain front on the return—the core of the trail lies in the woods and the meadows. Wildflowers light the grasses in spring, and the trees provide shade and a distinctive windblown song.

A variety of birds settle in the brush along the willow-bordered stream and pond to the right (north) as the trail begins its gentle descent toward the beach. Social trails cut right to the pond and left toward the homes through high desert sages; stay straight on the obvious path. A copse of aspen at the edge of the pond is a bird magnet.

Cross the stream below the pond via a curving boardwalk, then enter the first patch of woods. From here to the campground, the well-composed trail drops through meadows and rises through the woods in gentle undulations. Benches are placed along the track for rest and contemplation. In the distance the craggy peaks of the Desolation Wilderness cut the horizon.

The route ends at a signed trailhead in the Nevada Beach Campground. To reach the beach follow the campground road around to the right (north, then southwest) to sandy access trails near the restrooms. No dogs are allowed on the beach, but it is the perfect place to cool your feet before retracing your steps to the trailhead.

Miles and Directions

0.0 Start by heading down the wide dirt track toward Lake Tahoe.

0.1 Pass the pond. Ignore social trails that break right and left, staying on the main track.

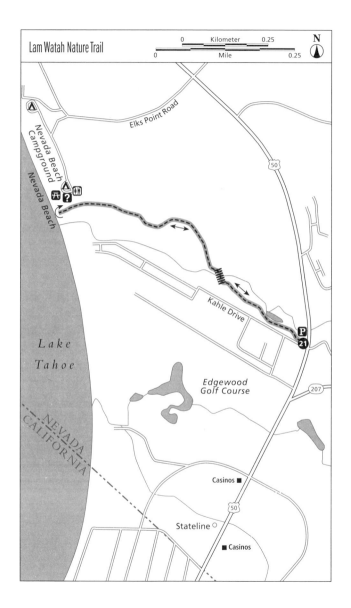

N

0   Kilometer   0.25

0   Mile   0.25

Elks Point Road

50

Nevada Beach Campground

Nevada Beach

Kahle Drive

P
21

Lake Tahoe

Edgewood Golf Course

207

NEVADA
CALIFORNIA

Casinos ■

Stateline ○

■ Casinos

50

0.3 Cross the boardwalk.

0.4 Trails merge in the woods; remain on the main track heading west toward the lakeshore.

1.0 Arrive at the Lam Watah trailhead in the campground. Follow the campground road around right (north), then left (southwest) to the sandy beach access by the restrooms.

1.1 Reach the beach, relax a while, then retrace your steps.

2.3 Arrive back at the trailhead.

22 Angora Lakes

Pack your towels and bring the kids: The Angora Lakes Trail is short, sweet, and lip-smacking good—the perfect introduction to hiking in the mountains around Lake Tahoe.

Distance: 1 mile out and back
Approximate hiking time: 45 minutes
Difficulty: Easy
Trail surface: Dirt access road
Best seasons: Summer and fall
Other trail users: Mountain bikers and the occasional automobile
Canine compatibility: Leashed dogs permitted; dogs may not swim in the lake
Fees and permits: Parking fee
Schedule: Hike the trail from sunrise to sunset daily. The resort is open daily from mid-June to mid-September.

Maps: USGS Echo Lakes (CA), but no map is necessary
Trail contact: USDA Forest Service Lake Tahoe Basin Management Unit, Forest Supervisor's Office, 35 College Dr., South Lake Tahoe, CA 96150; (530) 543-2600; www.fs.fed.us/r5/ltbmu
Other: Angora Lakes Resort offers day users access to the snack shack (where the lemonade is sold) and kayak and boat rentals. Cabins book well in advance; visit www.angoralakes resort.com or call (530) 541-2092 for more information.

Finding the trailhead: From the intersection of US 50 and CA 89 in South Lake Tahoe, go north on CA 89 for 3 miles to Fallen Leaf Lake Road. Turn left (west) onto Fallen Leaf Lake Road and go 2 miles to Tahoe Mountain Road. Turn left (southwest) onto Tahoe Mountain Road and follow it for 0.4 mile to unsigned FR 1214 (look for an open gate; the road appears to be dirt at the outset). Turn right (west) onto FR 1214 and travel 3 miles on the scenic, narrow, paved roadway to the parking area. The trailhead is beyond the gate

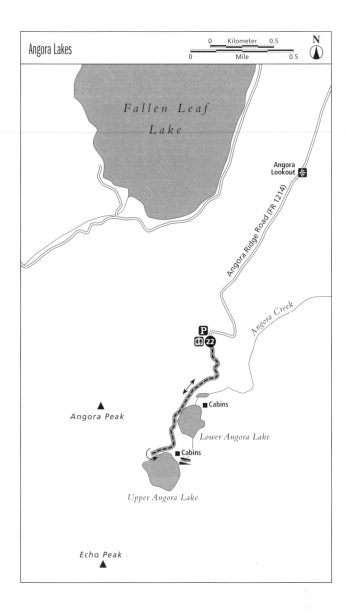

Angora Lakes

N

0   Kilometer   0.5
0   Mile   0.5

Fallen Leaf Lake

Angora Lookout

Angora Ridge Road (FR 1214)

Angora Creek

P

22

Angora Peak

Cabins

Lower Angora Lake

Cabins

Upper Angora Lake

Echo Peak

at the south end of the upper lot. Restrooms, information, and fee stations are in the lot. GPS: N38 52.261' / W120 03.788'

The Hike

After a short romp up a wide access road (with just enough elevation gain to get your heart pumping), you'll land on the sandy shores of Upper Angora Lake, replete with a spectacular alpine setting, cool water for swimming, rowboats for rent, and a snack bar that features some of the best lemonade money can buy. It's not a wilderness experience, but the hike has charm, and the destination, set among steep granite walls and featuring a narrow beach, is a dream.

Begin by following the access road as it loops in broad arcing turns up a boulder-strewn, forested hillside. After the short climb, the path flattens and is intersected by social paths that lead right (south) toward private residences on Lower Angora Lake. Stay left (southwest) on the main track, tracing the north shore of the lower lake.

An exceptionally brief climb leads to the snack bar and cabins on the eastern shores of Upper Angora Lake. The west and north shores are contained by black-streaked terraced cliffs spilling down from Echo and Angora Peaks. The beach hugs the north shore; stake out a patch of sand, sip some luscious fresh-squeezed lemonade, and enjoy.

Miles and Directions

- **0.0** Start by heading up on the broad, busy dirt track.
- **0.2** Reach Lower Angora Lake.
- **0.5** Rest on the shores of Upper Angora Lake, then retrace your steps.
- **1.0** Arrive back at the trailhead.

23 Pacific Crest Trail at Echo Lakes

This leg of the fabled Pacific Crest Trail stretches from the granite slabs above Lower Echo Lake to the forested shore of the Upper Echo Lake. The hiking is wonderfully easy and visually exciting, especially at the outset where the route skirts the granite outcrops at the base of Flagpole Peak.

Distance: 2.5 miles one way (with a boat taxi shuttle) or 5 miles out and back

Approximate hiking time: 1.5 hours one way or 3 hours out and back

Difficulty: Moderate due to trail length and rocky terrain

Trail surface: Dirt and rock singletrack

Best seasons: Summer and fall

Other trail users: None

Canine compatibility: Leashed dogs permitted

Fees and permits: There is no fee if you hike out and back; a fee is charged for the boat shuttle. You must fill out a free wilderness permit, available at the trailhead, if you hike into the wilderness area, regardless of whether you use the shuttle or not.

Schedule: The trail can be hiked sunrise to sunset daily. Boat shuttles are available until 6:00 p.m. in the summer months.

Maps: USGS Echo Lakes (CA); Tom Harrison Recreation Map of Lake Tahoe

Trail contact: USDA Forest Service Lake Tahoe Basin Management Unit, Forest Supervisor's Office, 35 College Dr., South Lake Tahoe, CA 96150; (530) 543-2600; www.fs .fed.us/r5/ltbmu

Finding the trailhead: From the junction of US 50 and CA 89 in South Lake Tahoe, drive west on US 50 for 10 miles, over Echo Summit, to a right (north) turn onto Johnson Pass Road (with sign). Go 0.5 mile on Johnson Pass Road to Echo Lakes Road. Turn left (north) onto Echo Lakes Road and drive 1.2 miles to the Echo Chalet. Parking can be tight; if no parking is available at the chalet, scout a spot along the road or in the upper parking lot, and walk the short distance down to the chalet and trailhead. Food, lodging, restrooms, and information are available at the trailhead. GPS: N38 50.085' / W120 02.611'

The Hike

The granite basin that holds Echo Lakes, at the edge of Desolation Wilderness and near the crest of the Sierra, provides a lovely setting for this easy stretch of the combined Pacific Crest Trail (PCT) and Tahoe Rim Trail (TRT). As you look down from the rocky path, the surface of the lower lake shimmers in the sun; the upper lake is mostly hidden from the trail by a dense evergreen forest that shades its shores. Ahead, to the north, the broad pass between Keiths Dome (on the northwest side) and Ralston Peak (on the southwest side) rises in a headwall of great silvery terraces, at once beckoning and imposing, hinting at the alpine treasures that lie above and beyond.

The trail begins at the southern end of the lower lake, crossing the causeway atop the dam and the bridge that spans the spillway. The trail switches back up the hill past trail signs to a trail intersection. Head left (north) on Pacific Crest Trail, which begins its traverse above the western shoreline by climbing through the manzanita onto granite slabs. The trail is etched in the bleached granite, narrow but well-traveled, about 200 feet above the surface of the navy blue water.

Not far beyond a section of trail that has been augmented with asphalt, pass above the first of many charming vacation cabins that line both lakes. Gentle climbing leads to a trail sign near some of those cabins, then two switchbacks lead

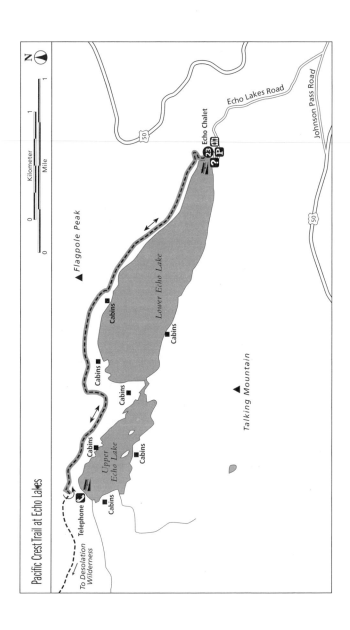

Pacific Crest Trail at Echo Lakes

up the steepest part of the hike, with the ascent moderating again as you approach the far reaches of the lower lake.

The route drops through a rocky, brushy section in the shadow of an overhanging slab streaked with black, gray, and orange. Climb through the gap between the two lakes, where the trail and bordering hillside is stained orange with iron that has oxidized in the rock.

The trail bends back to the north, offering brief views of the upper lake and the stony islands of the narrow passage between the two blue pools. An easy traverse along the wooded shores of the upper lake offers no views, but the dense forest shades a colorful understory of brush, grasses, and wildflowers that ring with birdcall.

Crest a small rise. A TAXI sign has been nailed to a big fir tree, where the narrow path to the boat dock branches off to the left (west). Drop about 50 yards to the boat dock where you can pick up the phone and call for the boat taxi—the swift ride across both lakes is a treat for kids of all ages. Or, if you choose, take a break on the dock overlooking the lake, then retrace your steps to the trailhead.

Miles and Directions

0.0 Start by crossing the dam at the south end of Lower Echo Lake. At the Tahoe Rim Trail/Pacific Crest Trail signs and map, head up and right, then around left (north) to parallel the lake shore.

0.3 Climb across a granite slab.

1.1 Pass a trail sign above a cluster of cabins. The trail switchbacks up the hillside.

1.6 Pass a black-streaked overhanging rock on the right, then the trail flattens alongside cabins.

2.0 Cross the red soils of the isthmus separating the upper and lower lakes. The lake views disappear.

2.3 Pass through an open woodland filled with wildflowers and birdsong.

2.5 At the ᴛᴀxɪ sign nailed onto the tree, turn left (west) and drop to the boat dock. This is the turnaround point for an out-and-back hike or the place to pick up the boat taxi.

5.0 Arrive back at the trailhead.

Options: The PCT and TRT continue into the high country, where a wonderland of lakes, including Lake Aloha, awaits.

24 Tahoe Rim Trail at Big Meadows

Experience the seductions of a mountain meadow on this rejuvenating high-country wander. A quick climb leads to the grassland, stuffed with wildflowers of different colors at different times. And, like buttercream icing on a chocolate cake, a river (okay, a gurgling creek) runs through it.

Distance: 2 miles out and back
Approximate hiking time: 1 hour
Difficulty: Easy
Trail surface: Dirt singletrack
Best seasons: Late spring, summer, fall
Other trail users: Mountain bikers, equestrians
Canine compatibility: Leashed dogs permitted
Fees and permits: None
Schedule: Sunrise to sunset daily

Maps: USGS Freel Peak and Echo Lake (CA); Tahoe Rim Trail map available at the trailhead
Trail contact: USDA Forest Service Lake Tahoe Basin Management Unit, Forest Supervisor's Office, 35 College Dr, South Lake Tahoe, CA 96150; (530) 543-2600; www.fs.fed.us/r5/ltbmu. Tahoe Rim Trail Association, 948 Incline Way, Incline Village, NV 89451; (775) 298-0233; www.tahoerimtrail.org

Finding the trailhead: From the intersection of US 50 and CA 89 in South Lake Tahoe, drive south on US 50/CA 89 for 4.7 miles to Meyers, where the two highways diverge. Turn left (southwest) onto CA 89, and go 5.1 miles to the signed Big Meadows trailhead on the left (north). Follow the short access road to the lower parking lot and the signed trailhead. Plenty of parking and an information signboard with maps, trash cans, and restrooms are at the trailhead. GPS: N38 47.316' / W120 00.044'

The Hike

Mountain meadows witness the passage of the seasons in magical ways. In springtime and early summer, wildflowers are the main attraction, clustered in pockets of red, purple, white, and yellow, and busy with butterflies and bees harvesting sweet nectars. By late summer and autumn the flower display has diminished, but a glistening gold spreads through grasses that have absorbed the warm hues of the summer sun. Even in winter, blanketed in thick snow, a mountain meadow is a calming, meditative place.

Big Meadows is all this, green and gold, easygoing and restful, delightful in all its incarnations.

The trail begins in the lower trailhead parking area, just beyond the information sign. Pass a blue and white Tahoe Rim Trail sign almost immediately; the trail runs alongside the highway until it climbs to the edge of the asphalt and crosses the road.

The path steepens on the other side of the pavement, climbing through a forest of stout mixed evergreens. Climb a log and granite staircase that makes it hard to comprehend that mountain bikers often ride the route. Highway noise filters through the forest, but the chatter of noisy Big Meadows Creek helps mask the sound.

The trail flattens as the highway noises fade; the boulder-strewn woodland is now full of birdsong and windsong. At the trail fork, go right (south), following the arrow that points to Meiss Meadow (aka Big Meadows); the left-hand trail leads to Scotts Lake.

Traverse a brief final stretch of woodland, then the world opens on the meadow. The path, worn into the turf, leads to a footbridge across the clear creek, then cuts a straight

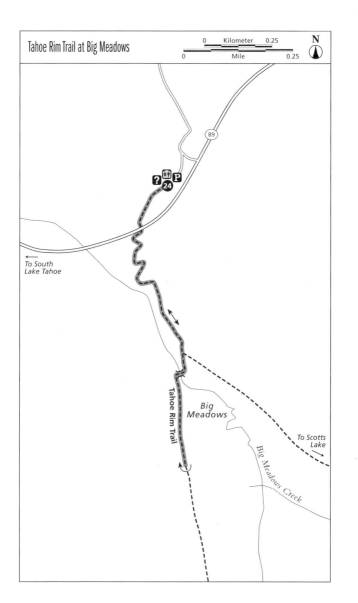

Tahoe Rim Trail at Big Meadows

Kilometer

Mile

N

To South
Lake Tahoe

Tahoe Rim Trail

Big
Meadows

To Scotts
Lake

Big Meadows Creek

line through the grasses and wildflowers to the dense forest that buffers the southern edge of the meadow and carpets the rolling mountains that cradle it.

The turnaround point is at the interface of the meadow and forest, though you can continue into the woodland. Sun-bleached stumps, once sturdy enough to provide restful seats and now cracked and rotting, mark the spot. Return as you came.

Miles and Directions

0.0 Start at the signed trailhead.

0.1 Cross CA 89.

0.6 At the trail intersection stay right (south) on the signed MEISS MEADOW trail (aka Big Meadows).

0.7 Reach the edge of the meadow.

1.0 Arrive at the turnaround point at the southwest edge of the meadow. Take a breather, than retrace your steps

2.0 Arrive back at the parking lot.

About the Author

Tracy Salcedo-Chourré has written more than twenty FalconGuides to destinations in California and Colorado, including *Hiking Lassen Volcanic National Park, Exploring California's Missions and Presidios, Exploring Point Reyes National Seashore and the Golden Gate National Recreation Area, Best Rail-Trails California,* and Best Easy Day Hikes guides to the San Francisco Bay Area, Lake Tahoe, Reno, Sacramento, Boulder, Denver, and Aspen. She is an editor, teacher, and soccer mom and lives with her husband, three sons, and a small menagerie of pets in California's Wine Country. You can learn more by visiting her Web page at the FalconGuides site, www.falcon.com/user/172.

WHAT'S SO SPECIAL ABOUT UNSPOILED, NATURAL PLACES?

Beauty   Solitude   Wildness   Freedom   Quiet   Adventure

Serenity   Inspiration   Wonder   Excitement

Relaxation   Challenge

There's a lot to love about our treasured public lands, and the reasons are different for each of us. Whatever your reasons are, the national **Leave No Trace** education program will help you discover special outdoor places, enjoy them, and preserve them—today and for those who follow. By practicing and passing along these simple principles, you can help protect the special places you love from being loved to death.

THE PRINCIPLES OF LEAVE NO TRACE

- Plan ahead and prepare
- Travel and camp on durable surfaces
- Dispose of waste properly
- Leave what you find
- Minimize campfire impacts
- Respect wildlife
- Be considerate of other visitors

Leave No Trace is a national nonprofit organization dedicated to teaching responsible outdoor recreation skills and ethics to everyone who enjoys spending time outdoors.

To learn more or to become a member, please visit us at www.LNT.org or call (800) 332-4100.

Leave No Trace, P.O. Box 997, Boulder, CO 80306